Denys Parsons was educated at Eton and the universities of Munich and London. He has been a research chemist, educational and industrial film-maker and a group manager at the National Research Development Corporation. From 1973 he was head of press and public relations at the British Library. He now combines a flourishing piano tuning business with writing, and translating and editing for technical translation bureaux.

He started collecting funny misprints as a schoolboy and his first book of them was published by Macdonald in 1952 after rejection by 12 other publishers; five more followed. His major work was the *Directory of Tunes*, published in 1975, and he also compiled an offbeat shopping guide *What's Where in London* which went into seven editions. Denys Parsons is married with two sons and lives in north London.

TOO FUNNY FOR WORDS

Denys Parsons

**Drawings by
ANTON**

Futura

A **Futura** Book

Copyright © this compilation Denys Parsons 1986

First published in Great Britain in 1986
by Futura Publications, a Division of
Macdonald & Co (Publishers) Ltd
London & Sydney
Reprinted 1987

ISBN 0 7088 3086 2

Typeset in Baskerville by
Fleet Graphics, Enfield, Middlesex
Printed and bound in Great Britain by
Collins, Glasgow

Futura Publications
A Division of
Macdonald & Co (Publishers) Ltd
Greater London House
Hampstead Road
London NW1 7QX

A BPCC plc Company

INTRODUCTION

A friend who was on a Unesco tour of duty in Phnom Penh had a letter from his wife in London: 'Peter is off colour and has carachi.' To the fond father of the boy of seven this was disturbing news. What was 'carachi?' The library and a local doctor couldn't help. Fortunately his wife's next letter was written in less straggly writing: 'Peter's earache is much better now.'

Over the last thirty years I have made a modest sum from the mistakes of other people. My speciality is collecting funny newspaper misprints and the like, and I began this as a schoolboy. Unconscious humour has always seemed to me by far the funniest type of humour. When we're faced with a manufactured joke we are being invited to laugh at the cleverness of the writer or illustrator. But when the mishap is unintentional we are not being pressured to laugh; it is *we* who are being clever – we saw the joke that was not supposed to be there,

FATHER OF TEN SHOT DEAD –
mistaken for a rabbit

The sub-editor who wrote that headline can scarcely be blamed, but another, who failed to appreciate the importance of word order, might be taken to task.

WOMAN HURT WHILE COOKING HER
HUSBAND'S DINNER IN A HORRIBLE
MANNER

And perhaps the following advertisement might have

been better without that comma: 'This appliance will reduce your hips, or bust.'

As my collection of hilarious items grew I began to fantasise. Choking with laughter over my latest find, I became convinced that a mischievous character, whom I named Gobfrey Shrdlu, was lurking at the elbows of tired journalists – sub-editors and compositors, causing moments of aberration and the perpetration of these grotesque errors. The name SHRDLU, by the way, I took from a set of keys on the compositor's Linotype machine – it corresponds to the QWERTYUIOP of the typewriter.

This book presents, in re-edited form, the material from three hardback titles published by Macdonald in the 1950s: *It Must Be True, Can It Be True?*, and *All Too True*. I had enormous fun collecting them, so here's hoping you and your friends will find my collection TOO FUNNY FOR WORDS.

I am grateful to Mr. John Yeoman for allowing me to use the witty drawings made by his late wife Antonia ('Anton').

Readers who are going to be responsible for arranging a wedding should take care that Gobfrey Shrdlu does not gate-crash the ceremony or reception. If he does, the effect on the report in the local paper is likely to be devastating.

The bride, who was given away by her father, wore a dress of pale bridegroom. She was attended by the hat, and carried a bouquet, the gift of the pink taffeta silk and a large dark blue bridegroom's two little nieces.

Kentish Paper

The bride wore a gown of white marquisette with finger-tip veil. She carried a white missile covered with orchids.

Baker (Oregon) Democrat-Herald

Francis Bellinghausen, of Stillwater, brother of the bride, was topped with a single white orchid.

Ponca City (Okla.) News

Here the couple stood, facing the floral setting and exchanged cows.

California Paper

Appropriate music was played on the organ by Mr. G.E. satin with pearl trimming. Her train was that on earth do dwell' and 'Father, now Thy grace extending.'

The bride was becomingly attired in white Good. The hymns sung were 'All people of silver lace, and she wore a tulle veil, which had been used at her mother's wedding.

Local Paper

The bride was attired in navy-blue georgette and hat to match, and carried a bouquet of roses and baby.

Iowa Paper

One of the first to arrive at the church was Lady D——, nearly attired in a dove-grey costume.

Bedford Paper

The bride looked charming. She carried a bouquet of white roses and carnations and the bridegroom.

Local Paper

The bride entered the church decorated with bowls of pink Dorothy Perkins roses, with Mr. Lawrence Palmer, brother of the bridegroom, who gave her away.

Natal Paper

The marriage took place at Salter's Road Methodist
Church, Gosforth, today, of Miss Gwendoline Dodds,
Gosforth, and Lieut. Frederick Dodds, of 6 Kensington
Avenue, daughter of Mr. and Mrs. E. Robinson, R.N.F.,
son of Mrs. E. Robinson, of 42 Blackwell Lane,
Robinson. The bride was Darlington, and the late Mr.
attended by Mrs. E.K. Rawlins and the best man was
Lieut. F. McCormack, R.N.F.

Northern Paper

The service was conducted by the Rev. ——. After
the Benedictine, Mr. and Mrs. —— sang 'I'll walk
beside you.'

Report of Wedding

The bride wore a gown of white sheer with lace
insects.

Cleveland Paper

Mrs. David Miller has a new baby boy at her
house. Dave is just as happy as if it was his.

Ohio Paper

*In the original edition I divided the items by subject, as above:
weddings, sport, crime, music etc. It now seems to me more
fun to present the greater part of them in higgledy-piggledy
order for your enjoyment. In family surroundings may I
strongly suggest that one of those present reads the items aloud.
Don't ask me why, but that seems to make them even funnier.*

At 6.45 p.m. at the Young People's meeting, there
will be a review of the first eight chapters of the Book
of the Acts. The review will be in the form of a base-
ball game.

Battle Creek (Michigan) Enquirer

If my mother were alive today to see shops opened and mixed bathing on the Sabbath, she would turn in her grave.

Letter in Irish Paper

STENOGRAPHER – five years legal experience, seeks permanent connections. DeLuxe model, good shape, many extras, used for pleasure spins by private owner. A real bargain. 522 E. Broad St.

Cleveland (Ohio) News

The competitors were in no way upset by the cold north-east wind blowing on the diving-board from the four corners of the earth.

Daily Mail

On Thursday a large band of rebels wearing uniforms, and fully equipped with rifles and ammunition, concentrated in the village of Kilmanagh, County Kilkenny. They bivouacked for some four hours behind a barricade composed of creamery cats.

Provincial Paper

For nearly five weeks Colonel Noivikov let his men through impenetrable thickets and impassable marshes, attacking and destroying the enemy.

Glasgow Paper

ARE YOU INVITED TO THE MAYOR'S
GARDEN PARTY?
If so, you will require the services
of the
HYGIENIC LAUNDRY

Advert. in Gloucestershire Echo

Our parents had gone there for a year or two to be near our grandmother on their return from their first visit to Europe, which had quite immediately followed my birth, which appears to have lasted some year and a half, and of which I shall have another word to say.

From 'A Small Boy and Others' by Henry James

When a sheep is seriously cut or otherwise injured, the sheep shall immediately report the fact to the person in charge of the shed.

Otago Daily Times

The gutted carcase of a deer was found yesterday afternoon near Fonthill Road. While investigating this, State Trooper Howard Johnson was bitten on the left arm by a dog owned by Miss Ann Lacko of Fonthill Road.

Police at the local sub-station said the dog would be let loose and Johnson tied up for ten days.

New Jersey Paper

Scores of people sitting on the peer heard him shout.

Seaside Paper

Mr. Jackson maintained that it was extraordinary that if he was only slightly dead deceased did not hear the lorry.

Bucks Paper

The police announce that dogs without dollars found wandering after 10 p.m. are liable to be destroyed.

Hong Kong Paper

The Wilson County Baptist Fifth Sunday meeting
will be held at Cedar Grove Baptist Church on March
30th.

Visitors from other churches will be spread on the
ground if weather permits.

Tennessee Paper

**SAN DIEGO, CALIFORNIA, DEC. 28.
MRS. R.S. WYGAL MAILED A FRUIT
CAKE TO HER SON ARINE SGT.
EDWARD R.W. RO MMMMM.
MMMMM. MM. MMM. M MMMMM.
MM. MMMM. MMM . . . . MMMMM . .
M. MMMM. M.MMMM. MMMM . . . .
MMM . . . . MMMMM.mmmmm.
MMMMMM . . . MMMM . . M.M.
MMMMM. MMM.MMMM . . . M. MM
MMMMM . . . M.MMMM.**

United Press message

***We do not tear your clothes
with machinery
We do it carefully by hand***

Sign in Laundry Window

A charming fire at 42 Western Rd., Brighton,
necessitated the calling of the Fire Brigade.

Brighton Paper

She raised her head, startled, and stared at a young boy who was smiling at her. Spread around her was a sun-flooded valley where buttercups nodded lazily in the summer breeze and tranquil cows chewed solemnly at her elbow.

Lady desires post; domesticated, fond of cooking children.

Weekly Paper

Drop hot cooked rice into hot soap by spoonfuls and you will have rice dumplings.

Indiana Paper

Mr. Jager, driving against Mr. Pollock from the first tee, pulled his ball into the press tent and ran under the flooring.

Dundee Courier

In carrying his bath right through the innings on Thursday for 125, A.O. Jones has made a brilliant start.

Irish Field

Make certain of getting the best of everything by sending to G - - - -s.

We advise you to buy the best, for even then it is not too good.

Capetown Outfitter's Advert.

There is a new name among the apothecaries of Roseau today. Messrs. Blank and Blank have opened a new business under the style THE ROSEAU PHARMACY. We sincerely wish the undertakers a full measure of prosperity.

The Dominica Chronicle

BARBED WIRE CLOTH for youngsters' suits; almost unwearable.

Advert. in Ladybrand Courant

LONELY LADY, 43, with little dog, seeks post.

Exeter Express and Echo

Bernard Colodney of 754 Mamaroneck Avenue was given a summons yesterday for permitting a dog to run at large after it was struck and killed in front of his address by a car.

White-Plains Reporter-Dispatch

THE DAFFODIL BAR – By a misprint this ball was stated to have been organised by the National Society of Cruelty to Animals. It should, of course, have been children not animals.

The Irish Independent

Stop and think for a moment. Many people are all run down, tired out and hardly able to drag about – don't know what's the matter with them. The answer, of course, is Blank's Cod Liver Extract, the great tissue builder.

Advert. in Lahore Civil and Military Gazette

Late that same evening after a vain search all round the village, Mary found the dog dead in the garden. She curried the body indoors.

Short Story

SIAMESE KITTENS, very good points and eyes; dam good pedigree.

Advert. in Daily Graphic

WANTED, new pair of football boots, for a good young Fox-terrier dog.

Advert. in Our Dogs

Dip your soiled face in alcohol, rinse it in the liquid and hang it straight out to dry. It may then be pressed.

Toronto Mail

Based on a lanolin combination, the suntan oil is readily absorbed by the skin. In a delightful shade of coffee with cream, it will not stain the clothes or the skin.

The results can be so severe as to scar the individual for life.

Houston Post

Mr. and Mrs. Charles L. Thompson and Mr. and Mrs. Russel Hatwick of Tampa will entertain an open house, Sunday, from three until tight.

Florida Paper

Dear Sirs,

My baby was so nervous that it nearly went into spams at every loud noise. I saw your advertisement and gave it T—— Syrup, and it is all over it.

A testimonial

EDINBURGH WOMEN AT THE WASH-TUB
REMARKABLE FIGURES

Edinburgh Evening News

Party who took green silk pyjamas from clothes line at No. 240 West 120th Street please return and no embarrassing exposure will be made on my part.

Oklahoma City News

CONGRATULATIONS to James and Christina Trencher on the birth of their daughter, their second child, on Friday at George Washington Hospital. The baby, to be called Eloise, is the daughter of the former Chilean Ambassador and Senora de M——.

Washington Post

The Hotel's bathroom has been enlarged and will hold over two hundred dancers.

Advert. in Colonial Paper

The match was unfinished owing to measles. Craghurst was compelled to scratch.

The Harrovian

JAMES GUNNINGHAM & CO.
DISPENSING CHEMISTS
We dispense with accuracy

Shop sign

You may imagine it is impossible to obtain a good, serviceable suit for 5 gns. Buy one from us and be convinced.

Advert. in Manchester Paper

Because there has been some misunderstanding as to which Mrs. Wood has been ill, we wish to tell readers of the Bulletin that it is Mrs. Lucille Wood and not Mrs. Lucille Wood. There, that will clear that up!

Church Bulletin

JACK'S LAUNDRY
Leave your clothes here, ladies, and spend the afternoon having a good time.

Advert. in New Mexico Paper

It is not considered polite to tear bits off your beard and put them in your soup.

Etiquette Book

After Governor Baldridge watched the lion perform, he was taken to Main Street and fed twenty-five pounds of raw meat in front of the Fox Theatre.

Idaho Statesman

AN ADMIRAL NOW RECEIVES $8,000 PLUS $2,000 IN LOVING ALLOWANCES

U.P. Press Dispatch

Colleen has four brothers and two sisters, all contest winners of one sort or another. Her parents are both tall. Her father, ugh, is an inventor of several bull-dozer attachments.

The Journal-American

For about a year Walton has been manager of the Liv.-Pak Corporation, a firm that ships live lobsters to customers packed in ice.

Boston Post

All are gone except the indefatigable Mr. C.——,
who manages to rise like a Felix from the ashes of any
financial disaster.

Sussex Paper

Captain Rogers shot a pariah dog in the grounds of
the Terrace a few days ago and was destroyed in the
bazaar the following morning.

The Pioneer

Blue gentleman's serge coat and skirt, latest, worn
once, 5 ½ gns.

The Lady

Then it spread to Liz, who clapped a hand over her
mouth above blue eyes that watered with silent
laughter.

From 'Nothing' by Henry Green

'You were courting this young lady in one breath
and setting fire to her car in the next,' said Judge D.

Daily Mail

Owing to the steering gear going wrong, the car ran
up on the fence and capsized. The driver was
removed to —— Infirmary for treatment under a
cosmetic.

Irish Paper

Enclosed please find birth certificate of a child born
to above member of our staff for purposes of tax
adjustment.

Letter to Inland Revenue

This was in striking contrast to the scene outside, where all was bright and animate, the countryside looking resplendent and at its best, in the early autumn garbage.

Bedfordshire Standard

We have the same eggs for sale that we had last winter. Come and see us.

Pyote (Oklahoma) Clarion

There was little Ernest Hunter, whose indescribable hat covered a head that must have knocked around the world considerably before he found it.

The Clarion

Woman wants cleaning three days a week.

Advert. in Manchester Guardian

LOST- between Kneeland St. and Hotel Statler, 2-headed man's snake ring with green and red stones. Reward.

Advert. in Boston Herald

Pair of ladies found by William Hallet at the Stroudsburg Methodist Church a week ago may be secured by owner by calling at the church and paying for this ad.

Stroudsburg (Pa.) Record

White muslin Blouse; new pointed joke. Each Rs 4/4.

Bombay Catalogue

Then they waved to their friends with one hand and chewed sandwiches with the other.

Norfolk Paper

She sat huddled in a chair, covering her ears with crossed legs.

Short Story

LOST. Evening frock and undergarments with Gladys H—— inside. Finder rewarded.

Kentucky Paper

The doctor and his wife, it was stated, today, were often seen riding in a car which plunged 300 feet into the sea off Beachy Head.

The Star

L—— and C—— sit face to face across two desks pushed together and the visitor is seated halfway between them.

N. Y. Herald Tribune

He was dirty and his eyes, bloodshot from loss of sleep, were embedded in a fortnight's growth of beard.

Reader's Digest Companion

My teeth were chattering as with a fever-chill, when they all tumbled out.

The Story Teller

COPS CAN FIND 96.2% OF ANYBODY LOST IN NEW YORK CITY

Mexico City Herald

Dr. Garside said that after the accident Williams did several of the tests quite well. Williams told him he had been to a very good dinner and had a good deal to drink at it. He was certain that his car had touched nothing.

Bristol Evening Post

The font so generously presented by Mrs. Smith will be set in position at the East End of the church. Babies may now be baptised at both ends.

Surrey Paper

The announcement that the Vicar has raided a fund for the support of the unfortunate man's wife will be welcomed by all.

Derby Paper

'I was throwing the snowball at some Scouts, not at the policeman,' said the boy, pleading not guilty today to a charge of insulting behaviour.

'Nobody wants you to stop playing snowballs – it is a grand game – but you must now throw them at policemen,' said the magistrate.

The Star

W.C.T.U. monthly meeting at Boulevard Church, 1.30 p.m. Monday October 9th. The meeting will be gin with prayer.

California Church Programme

The Vicar will give a short address, whilst the anthem will be 'The Two Acrobats'.

Blackpool Times

FORTHCOMING HANDBOOK

HOW I CAN GET AN OLD AGE PENSION

In six volumes. Half-morocco,
143 woodcuts.

Publisher's announcement

Mr. and Mrs. Benny Croset announce the birth of
a little son which arrived on the 5.15 last Thursday.

West Union (Oregon) People's Defender

The increase in number and percentage of autopsies is a tribute to the energy and zeal of the hospital staff in general and to the geniality and personal charm of our chief resident Dr. George Grainier.

Annual Report of a Connecticut Hospital

On making enquiries at the Hospital this afternoon, we learnt that the deceased is as well as can be expected.

Jersey Evening Post

Ensign and Mrs. William A. Clark have announced the girth of a son, Kenneth William, on Oct. 6th at Neenah, Wisconsin.

Montclair (New Jersey) Times

Mr. and Mrs. —— of Duke Hill are the parents of any infant daughter born Thursday.

Illinois Paper

Dr. W.T. —— read an interesting paper on 'Idiots from Birth'. There were over two hundred present.

Surrey Paper

BOREHAM. The offertories and the proceeds of the sale of girls together amounting to just over £12 were given to the London Missionary Society.

Essex Weekly News

In accordance with his annual custom, an unknown benefactor walked into the cashier's office of the Church Army last week, handed over a cheque for £500 and left without waiting for thanks.

As great quantities of such parasites are about at this season, it may be useful to give a few hints as to how to exterminate them.

Western Daily Press

The appeal of Morris Hindle against removal from the register was dismissed. Hindle is a painter and decorator, and part-time Jehovah's fish-retailer, Kendal.

Manchester Guardian

Two women were fined £5 or 14 days for throwing stones at Mr. John Burn's residence, and missing.

Western Morning News

Knocked down and badly injured by a motor-car in London Road, Kingston, what is described as a sea-lion 8 ft. long, weighing about 6 cwt. has been washed ashore near Fowey, Cornwall.

London Evening Paper

The General Committee and all the clergy and ministers (as well as the choir) are invited to sit on the orchestra.

West Country Paper

The Rev. W.L. Johnson will start for his annual holiday on June 13th. He therefore asks that the Missionary Boxes be returned to him not later than June 10th.

Parish Magazine

For some informality in front of the Durham goal posts, Gamon had a free kick allowed, but he made a wretched attempt with him to shake hands and say good-bye, for he was later.

Yorkshire Post

The Transvaal team for the match against Western Province today will not, it is stated, be chosen until tomorrow morning.

Rand Daily Mail

SHEFFIELD MAN'S MACHINE STRUCK TELEPHONE POLE BOTH IN HOSPITAL

Sheffield Paper

'Good,' muttered Armand Roche to himself, hiding a smile beneath the false black beard which he always carried in his portmanteau in case of an emergency.

Short story

Old Shrdlu has plenty of imagination. He delights in creating new people – 'people we never met' is what I call this facet of Shrdlu's activity.

GRAND CLASSICAL LANDSCAPE. By Deline-avit after Pietro de Cortona, the only landscape done by that old Master.

Art-dealer's Catalogue

The scheduled concert at the Boston Museum of Fine Arts this afternoon has been cancelled. It was to have featured Viola da Gamba and her harpsichord.

Boston Post

SALE of excellent household furniture, piano, and marble bas relief of the 14th Century, by Don A. Tello.

Chester Observer

Both the long jump and the high jump were won by Victor Ludorum.

Bedford Paper

Carl V. Hartley, 47-year-old veteran of both World Wars was awaiting arraignment today on charges of beheading his wife. As he waited he told McCabre jokes in his jail cell.

Newark News

Mrs. Robert Lee Brown of Ithaca was organist, playing 'Clair de Lune', 'At Dawing', 'To a Wild Rose', and 'On Don Tino'.

Ithaca (Mich.) Gratiot County Herald

Marble top dresser, walnut hall tree, bevel mirror, and J.A. Cobean 3-piece living room suite.

Shreveport (Louisiana) Times

We have printed, verbatim, all that Phillimore gives on the subject. Nor has Phillimore rested his facts on Prideaux alone. He quotes Ibid as his authority for paragraphs 3 and 4, both of which paragraphs confirm paragraph 2 based on Prideaux.

Nottingham Daily Express

27

Just to keep the record straight, it was the famous Whistler's Mother, not Hitler's, that was exhibited at the recent meeting of Pleasantville Methodists. There is nothing to be gained in trying to explain how the error occurred.

Titusville (Pa.) Herald

Taking the size of the average family as 4 – that is, father, mother, and 2 children, it is clear that 560,000 of the inhabitants of Berlin sleep in one room.

Tägliche Rundschau

Further outlook: some rain, becoming milk later

Yorkshire Paper

Dr. Cook's telegram to M. Lecointe states definitely that he reached the North Pole on the date mentioned above, and that he discovered land to the northward.

Daily Telegraph

Inventor wishing to sell his parents on reasonable terms, invites inquiries.

Daily Paper

Can you advise me what can be done to rid my house of earwigs? Last year we were alive with them. We used to find them on our bed, and used to run down the wall and across the table at mealtimes.

Amateur Gardening

Keeping all food under cover is the first step towards ridding the house of aunts.

Albany Journal

The electrical equipment of the car is so arranged that the mere fact of wishing to inspect any of the high tension apparatus causes the whole of this to be connected to earth and thus made safe.

Railway News

Whenever eggs are cheap the fowls yield a fair supply, and when they become dear production stops.

Pall Mall Gazette

No medicine is of any avail in this complaint. As it is contagious you should not put another bird into the same cage until it has been thoroughly disinfected by baking or boiling.

Bazaar, Exchange & Mart

'You look a bit washed out, Bill,' said Doreen. She walked across the room and put her arm through him.

Novelette

Andy let out a long, drawn-in breath.

Saturday Evening Post

It is much rarer for a woman to marry outside her own class than it is for a man.

Black and White

Dr. Charles Darwin lived just long enough to receive the admiring tributes of the whale community.

Manchester Evening News

His disappointment was keen, yet in after days he looked upon the evening as that date on which he burst from the chrysalis and became a caterpillar.

Grand Magazine

The month's severest storm damage exceeded £4,000,000, over half of which was caused by hail. A single hailstone caused crop and property damage of $1,500,000 in Colorado Springs.

U.S. Weather Bureau Report

Tomorrow we may expect N.E. winds, reaching a gal in exposed places.

Provincial Paper

The large comet was seen by a resident in the heavens in the direction of the Forest.

Football Echo

Kuida's skull was fractured and he was not given a chance to live by the attending physician.

Ontario (Calif.) Daily Report

Among the side-reactions of this mercurial drug the most important is the death of the patient shortly after the injection.

New York State Medical Journal

Mr. Samuel added that the number of new over-head wires would be comparatively small, and placed underground.

Daily Graphic

30

Beginning in the winter of 1938 Dr. Ewing and his associates, working on the deep-sea research vessel Atlantis, began to experiment with underwear photography.

New York Times

TODAY by general request – Farewell Concert of the Hungarian Symphony Orchestra.

Munich Paper

Dear Member,
  Just a reminder that the fourth Friday noon of February is next Monday, February 28th.

Church Circular

There will be a procession next Sunday afternoon in the grounds of the Monastery; but if it rains in the afternoon, the procession will take place in the morning.

Notice in Irish Church

London, July 14th – Mrs. Annie Besant, eighty-year-old theosophist, was confined to bed today at the home of friends at Wimbledon. A severe child forced her to cancel all lecture engagements.

Houston Chronicle

Children found straying will be taken to the Lion House.

Notice in Zoo

John Sewell, a public health department inspector, said he visited the potted meat manufacturer and found it was prepared by chopping tinned boiled beef to which spices, gelatine, and boiling water were added. The mixture was made up in ten pound notes.

Daily Paper

32

Mrs. Frank Bundage received a long-distance message on Saturday evening informing her of the birth of a baby son, born Saturday afternoon at their home in St. Paul. The baby weighed 8lb. 9 oz.

Iowa Paper

The Nebraska legislature was asked to enact a law providing annulment of marriages of all couples who do not within three years after the wedding have one or more children by Representative Hines, Democrat of Omaha, who is a bachelor.

Radio News aboard U.S.S. Pennsylvania

High as the goal-bar this effort came skimming along, with every eye of the vast throng watching its progress on tiptoe.

Glasgow News

BALLOON RACE
SEVEN COMPETITORS FALL OUT

Edinburgh Evening Dispatch

Jeffries is not old, but he finds difficulty in reducing his portly waist to the dimensions of the prize-ring.

Daily Telegraph

For those who like watching trains, as I occasionally do, the Cornish Riviera Express passes through a halt a couple of miles away. And there are fishermen by the canal, running alongside the railway, willing to talk about pike.

from 'Wiltshire Harvest' by H.H. Bashford

Westward Ho! is a long course, and golfers who can hit the ball into the air and make it stay there should reap the advantage of their power.

Daily Telegraph

The first three balls yielded four runs. Then the bowler took a very long swift run – and bit the off stump.

Yorkshire Paper

He had been aware from the first that she was unusually attractive; now, in her dark green dress with the low-cut, rounded neckline, he saw that she had lovely legs.

from 'The Jade Venus' by G.H. Coxe

Rosmead was perfectly happy. He loved this woman with a great and growling love.

People's Friend

SEVENTEEN-YEAR LOCUSTS TO APPEAR NEXT SUMMER

State collee, Pa. Dec. 11 – The 17-yearg lgocgugst is due to appear agaginngg gnext summer, according to C.H. Hadley, Jr., an entemo-legeggggbmn TTMMggggborr . . . jEas logist at the Pennsylvania State College.

Erie Daily Times

Notice in Spanish Hotel

When logging in, do not use the word 'log' as a verb. This is an incorrect usage.

Army Navy Manual

On several occasions the thick end of the divining-rod rose up and struck the operator on the head. On these spots, he asserted, water would be found fifty feet down.

Daily Mirror

Over the range from about 450 degrees centigrade to upwards of 500 degrees centigrade, the coal passes through a phase of elasticity during which it can be moulded between the fingers like putty.

The Elements of Fuel Technology

Externally the design is modern, and internally the treatment is somewhat severe, as is usual in a hospital.

Daily Telegraph

Well-built modern house in 2 excellent self-contained flats. An opportunity not to be missed. Bath vacant in the early spring.

Gloucester Echo

It is stressed that these are not 'ordinary' plots, but really unique sites that cannot help but fail to appeal to the discerning purchaser.

Advert. in The Observer

She was sorry she had agreed to sleep in the haunted house, because all night long she was troubled by strange whiskers in her ear.

Serial Story

The bridegroom travelled in a two-piece clerical gray angora, striped with red and beige, worn with a black Robin Hood hat, trimmed with red.

Essex Paper

Until further notice, no steam-roller, steam-wagon, heavy lorry, or charabanc, will be allowed to run over the bride.

Bedford Paper

Mr. Richards had two daughters, Ethel Mary and Gwendoline Florence. To the former he left an annuity of £200 so long as she remained a sprinter.

South Wales Echo

Two or three models of such planes are already on the market, purchasable at $3,000 or thereabouts, either on the instalment plan, so much down, or else crash on delivery, but they are likely to drop, we understand.

New York Times

It was a most beautiful catch by Hutchings in the deep field on the leg side that dismissed Mr. Sprot. The tree which stands in the ground was too near to be pleasant, and Mr. Hutchings had to run back quickly and held it over his head.

The Times

After burning fiercely for an hour and a half firemen gained the upper hand.

Globe

TREATED LIKE DOG BY WIFE
HUSBAND COOKED FOR 30 YEARS

Daily Telegraph

In one Kentish orchard a single frosty night about a month ago decimated the currants by as much as 80 per cent.

Daily Mail

The County Council's veterinary inspector yesterday certified that death was due to anthrax, and was cremated by the police.

Yorkshire Post

Tradition says that the aborigines of the Patagonian region bathed their infants in icy water to toughen them. The aborigines are now extinct.

Philadelphia Enquirer

Basically there are few psychological differences between mule and female.

Weekly Paper

A HOSPITAL SPOKESMAN SAID HIS
CONDITION IS 'CATISFAMTORY'

News Wire to Chicago Daily News

FOR SALE, Doctor's sailing dinghy and accessories. Doctor no further use.

Yorkshire Paper

The marksmanship of the headquarters company is highly satisfactory and the shooting of the regimental sergeant-major was especially praiseworthy.

Daily Express

Miss Sutton struck out in all directions, and the nurses called for help. However, when Dr. Jacklin arrived she had been overpowdered.

Short Story

As a pioneer and professional man Dr. Bancky was out in front. Fifty-nine years he practised medicine, being responsible for most of the babies born in the community.

Pomeroy (Ohio) Democrat

Travelling in a becoming suit of Copenhagen blue with hat to match, the newlyweds left on the Duluth train.

Canadian Paper

Mortimer glanced at the people awaiting him in the hotel lounge and realised that he would have to put his bride in his pocket.

Serial Story

EGGS FOR HATCHING
FROM DAY-OLD CHICKS

Local Paper

About 3 a.m. a fire broke out in the back part of the premises of Messrs Blank, sausage and potted meat makers. Several horses were rescued.

The Star

The Countess of H—— was in invisible green velvet, with a black extinguisher hat.

The Standard.

For nearly three-quarters of an hour the fire blazed without any real abatement, and it was only when it had burned itself out that there was any real diminution of the intensity of the flames.

Dundee Advertiser

If your complexion is inclined to be dull and lifeless, don't despair. Try using a little varnishing cream regularly and you will be surprised at the result.

Woman's Paper

STRADIVARIUS VIOLIN FOR SALE CHEAP
Almost New.

Advert. in The All-STORY Magazine

Dancers are asked to wear at least some suggestion of a costume, if only a bandanna or for girls a big hair bow, to get into the spirit of the party.

Michigan Daily

Miss Crichton pluckily extinguished the blaze while Herr Eckold pulled the orchestra through a difficult passage.

Daily Express

Farmer S—— wishes to thank sincerely all those who assisted in the burning of his barn.

Suhler Intelligenz-Blatt.

'Ever green' was Sir Joseph Sykes Rymer's jocular reference to the new Lord Mayor and Lady in his speech proposing the election of the Lord Mayor, and not 'very green', as given in our issue of yesterday.

Yorkshire Herald

Oklahoma Papa

Para. 27b. Men employed on quasi-clerical nature should not be provided with any clothing.

Post Office Magazine

I only wish at the present moment I could convert myself into a doormouse till the genial weather arrives, and I daresay many of my readers would warmly welcome such a proposition.

The Graphic

Recent tests conducted by a zoologist prove that grasshoppers hear with their legs. In all cases the insects hopped when a tuning fork was sounded nearby. There was no reaction to this stimulus, however, when the insects' legs had been removed.

Corning Glass Works Magazine

To prevent a little girl's hair-slide from constantly slipping, put an elastic band or a piece of bicycle valve tubing round the under arm, opposite the teeth.

Woman's Illustrated

The carpet is your children's playground. Have them beaten or shampooed by our improved method.

Tradesman's Circular

The bridegroom's mother wore pale gray chiffon with V neck, short sleeves, and skirt having a cascade down at the front. With it she wore Harvard University with the Head of the division of chemistry, and returned to Cleveland only a few days ago.

Cleveland Paper

An exciting fire broke out yesterday on the premises of the Society for Promoting Christian Knowledge in Northumberland Avenue.

Daily Mirror

**DON'T KILL YOUR WIFE WITH WORK
LET ELECTRICITY DO IT**

Poster in Willesden

Wanted, Gentlewoman a few days old.

Advert. in The Lady

Captain Guest, Mr. Winston Churchill, and the other men worked the little fire engines which were kept at the house in their pyjamas.

Weekly Dispatch

Once while still in Russia, I saw a pair of slacks illustrated in an American magazine and made a pair like them for my vacation. When I made my entrance at the resort in them the Manager requested that they be removed.

The American Magazine

Dir Madman,
    have heard has you are in want of a maid and has I am in want of a place has maid would like to give you a trail.

Letter to prospective employer

Mrs. Thomas Jenning's classes for children of pre-kindergarten age will be resumed on Mondays, Wednesdays and Fridays, from 9 to 12 o'clock. A slight smack will be served about 10.30.

Connecticut Paper

An assistant master of the Bromley Road Schools submitted an application for leave of absence in order to attend a special vaccination course in geography.

Beckenham Journal

An English Government requires holiday engagement for six weeks.

Advert. in Buenos Aires Standard

Sir,

It gives me great pleasure to be able to tender you my good wishes for the future progress of your most popular morning paper, The Yorkshire Observer, without which I should not be satisfied, for it is half of my breakfast.

Letter in Yorkshire Observer

Lord X will be Peggy's fifth husband. In her matrimonial ventures she has been a countess but she never has been a lady.

Syracuse Journal

The easiest way to clean a cereal cooker is to turn it upside down in a pan of white flannel laid with the soft side on the inside and quilted on the machine.

Oxford Times

Adjoining the kitchen department is the store room, containing a large refrigerator with separate compartments for meats, poultry and fish, and a small compartment for the household clerk.

Englishman

HONOURABLE LADY would give conversation to foreigners. Moderate retribution.

Daily Paper

To emphasise the shape of the eyes, pencil in a fine brown line actually following the growth of the lashes. Mascara must be made into a nice creamy consistency and lower lashes made up as well with lemon curd and ice the top with lemon water icing, or sprinkle icing sugar on top.

Greenock Telegraph

Rev. F.R. Smith, a superintendent of the Lutheran Inner Mission, is attending a refresher course at Yale University's School of Alcohol Studies this week.

Dayton (Ohio) Herald

Word was received last week that Mrs. Gertrude Higgins, teacher of the 36th Street School, was severely bitten by a dog on the school grounds. Principal Gail Mahoney observed that it could just as easily have been a child.

Los Angeles South-West News-Press

The Bishop of Bristol was the sole occupant of the Episcopal Bench. He, having said prayers, stayed for the event of the day. The other Lords just looked in, swore, and went out again.

Irish Times

The crisis in Persia is dealt with by a Special Correspondent.

Daily Telegraph

As at the last election, it has once again stuck to its old colours. (Loud cheers and cries of 'Good old True Gloucester (cheers and cries of 'Good old Glouloucester – (Cheers, and cries of 'ood old loucester').

Weekly Paper

Meetings everywhere are crowded out . . . Not only that, but luke-warm sympathisers are burning red-hot enthusiasts.

The Clarion

It is reported from Bedfordshire that the Foreign Secretary, who is undergoing treatment, has had a less restful night. Swine fever has broken out.

Evening Standard

After all, we are largely as nature made us, and Governor Smith's smile was born with him, just as were his liking for children and his derby hat.

Omaha Evening World-Herald

45

Mr. Jones is wrong to suggest that I support the rich against the poor. To the Christian there is no class distinction – that idea was largely concocted by the working classes.

Letter in Reynolds News

The German Autumn Naval Manoeuvres will be confined to the Baltic Main Colliery near Sheffield.

Bath Herald

General McNarney, 58, former U.S. troop commander in Europe and at one time acting Supreme Allied Commander in the Mediterranean, is mentioned as likely to get a new NATO key job. It is designed to break production and supply bottle-necks.

Daily Mail

3.   Paragraph 56A. In line 2, after *Sunday* for *rice*, and in line 3 after *Thursday* for *sago*, substitute *blanc-mange* in each case.

Army Orders

Railway tickets of the Sunday Route March will be issued at drill hall on Wednesday; members who cannot attend please apply to Cr-Sergt, stating which line they travel by.

Rifle Brigade Battalion Orders

Prosecutor Charles Bell asked all the prospective jurors if they would inflict the death penalty 'if the evidence warranted it'. Those who said they were opposed to capital punishment under any circumstances were executed.

Cincinnati Times Star

POLICE DISBELIEVE A NAVAL STOKER WHO SAYS HE IS NOT DEAD

Daily Paper

In a collision of autos on Sylvan Street, a Ford sedan sustained a cut on the nose and bruise on the leg but declined medical aid.

Malden (Mass.) Evening News

LADY, SHORTHAND TYPIST, desires change; experience with criminal solicitor.

Manchester Guardian

Mayor Bonnet reported $3,456.00 collected as fines and costs in his Court during the month of May.

Building Commissioner Smith reported $82.50 collected by him for permits from April 16th to May 21st.

Both the Mayor and the Commissioner have left for Canada for a short vacation.

Bogota (Texas) News

CONGRESS SPLIT ON QUESTION OF CONGRESS SPLIT

Los Angeles Daily Journal

If you were writing a letter to a member of the Cabinet of the United States, how would you address him?

'My dead Mr. Secretary,' is the most acceptable form of address.

Cleveland Press

Upon the River Committee reporting that they could not recommend the adoption of the Surveyor's estimate of £26 for refacing the Town Clerk, Councillor Patmore said it seemed altogether out of all proportion.

Lymington & South Hants Chronicle

A local Italian, on being asked whether he had been summoned home for military service replied that he was a 'crystalised' Englishman. After a few moments of mental research his interrogator came to the conclusion that what the descendant of the Romans meant was 'nationalised'.

Rothesay Express

He smiled and let his gaze fall to hers, so that her cheek began to glow. Ecstatically she waited until his mouth slowly neared her own. She knew only one thing:
rdoeniadtrdgoveniardgoverdgovnrdgog.

Badische Presse

DEAR MISS DIX – A certain man has asked me to marry him, and I do not know whether to say 'yes or ETAOIN N N'

Miss Anxious
Tampa Tribune

Alderman—— stated that he had recently had a drink of the beer to test it. If the beer had been intoxicaty, he would certainly nog have ben ytsre uw lubsicating . . .

Canadian Paper

Lassalle fell in love in a few moments, carried the woman of his choice down exactly three flights of stairs, and then, as though his intellect had interfered to dampen his emotions, he let the whole matter drop.

from 'Genius and Character' by Emil Ludwig

Mr. and Mrs. John Beverlin are rejoicing over an eight-pound daughter, their sixth child since last Saturday.

Illinois Paper

A son was born to Mr. and Mrs. William Kleintop, Leigh Avenue, during the past week. Congratulations, Pete!

Palmerton (Pennsylvania) Press

Snow piled deep in the Scottish Highlands and England's lake district and blocked Russia's railroads.

New York Times

Club members are requested not to drive their cars into the club garage when it is full.

Notice at Irish Golf Course

Earlier the same afternoon Mrs. Jackson slipped off a bus and bruised a ship.

Uxbridge Weekly Post

George Grant is the proud possessor of a brand new Chevrolet sedan and also a new wife, having traded in the old one for which he received a liberal allowance.

The Logan (Ohio) Republican

FORT WORTH (AP). The Civil Aeronautics Board has applications on file for extensions of airline service to 723 cuties, many of them in Texas.

Texas Paper

The Christening ceremony was performed by Lady Maclay, wife of the Shipping Controller. Thousands of people saw her go down the ways, and cheers were raised as she took the water without the slightest hitch.

Daily News

In the next compartment was the wife of a prominent politician, off to the Riviera. Her husband, seeing her off, looked wistfully after the train as it pulled out of the station with its heavy load.

Daily Mail

Alderman Johnston moved that pending the passing of the street by-law, that all vehicles on Columbia Street be required to keep to the left going up and to the right going down.

The British Columbian

Mr. John Trimble, of the George Washington University, said that they had found England a wonderful country, especially the cathedrals. When he stood in Westminster Abbey he had really thought he was in heaven until he turned round and saw his colleagues standing by his side.

Provincial Daily

Mr. T—— sang with great feeling; 'Relieve me of all those endearing young charms.'

Sussex Paper

From first to last the grip that he maintained over his large audience was shown by the keen attention with which they hung upon his words and the deep silence with which their bursts of silence alternated.

Westminster Gazette

Recent animals at the Grand Hotel include Mr. and Mrs. S——.

Buenos Aires Paper

To create a scene when motoring over a careless cyclist or pedestrian, shows lack of control and good manners.

Evening Paper

FOR SALE. 9 h.p. 2 cylinder Clement, tonneau body for 4 . . . Owner getting larger.

Exchange and Mart

Party to leave bus station, bus No. 18. Alight at Sea Corner, Highcliffe, and proceed along shore. Tea at Barton-on-sea. Small chisels advised.

Bournemouth Natural Science Society Programme

That morning at the station was really agony. The scone will always remain in my memory.

Berkshire Paper

This place is the preferred resort for those wanting solitude. People searching for such solitude are in fact flocking here from all corners of the globe.

Swiss Resort Prospectus

Both the bandsmen and conductor had many adventures abroad, and the best of them was one in Sweden, when charming maids, on bringing coffee and cakes to their bedrooms in the early morning, removed their clothes. The alarmed salvationists were completely at a loss – until the raiders returned the garments carefully brushed and pressed.

The Star

Turrou's own life as fantastic as any case he ever worked on. His father, a French musician, died two years before he was born.

Magazine Article

Mrs. Robert M. Hitch, President of the Poetry Society, is expecting an unusually large attendance. There will be no original poems read at the meeting tonight by members.

Savannah (Georgia) Evening Press

Mrs. Grace Wright is being wired for electricity, which will be a great improvement and add considerably to her value to the community.

Medina Sentinel

The Bishop of —— who was enjoying the balmy morning driving his car, after a laborious Sunday, gave the hounds a 'view halloa' when the second fox broke, and the gallant Master rewarded his Lordship with the brush when hounds rolled him over.

Provincial Paper

Gobfrey Shrdlu can make his presence felt in any part of a newspaper, but possibly most embarrassing for editors is his perverse and malign interest in the answers to readers column.

Q.   What is the derivation and meaning of the name Erwin?

A.   It is English from the Anglo-Saxon and means Tarriff Act of 1909.

Columbus (Ohio) Citizen

Q.   How may slightly soiled playing cards be cleaned?

A.   They are made by stringing pieces of meat, quarters of onions, and two-inch pieces of bacon on sticks and broiling them over coals.

American Magazine

Q.   What does the thread count printed on the label of bed sheets and pillowcases indicate?

A.   The massacre of Ford Mickinac in 1763 by Chief Pontiac of the Ottawas.

Columbus (Ohio) Citizen

The Tasmanian wolf is striped like a tiger, has a tail like a rat, is a relative of opossums, and is the youngest man ever to be president of the United States.

Bridgewater (Conn.) Telegram

Q. How can you tell the age of a snake?
A. It is extremely difficult to tell the age of a snake unless you know exactly when it is born.

Detroit News

Q. Please give the prayer by Robert Louis Stevenson, beginning: 'The day returns . . .'
A. It is as follows: 'The day returns and brings us the petty round of irritating concerns and cuties . . .'

Wisconsin Paper

Q. What should a man call his wife when introducing her to his employer?
A. 'Mrs. Allen'.

California Paper

Q. What is the best method of cooking eggs to preserve the most vitamins?
A. Experiments have led to the conclusion that the best method of cooking eggs for vitamin retention is scrambling, followed by boiling and frying.

Boston Traveler

Q. What is the origin of the word 'Miami'?
A. From the French spelling of the Indian word 'Maumee', meaning 'Miami'.

Florida Grower

54

Q.   When does the Navy consider a man to be 38 years of age?
A.   The Navy considers a man to be 38 on his 28th birthday.

Stockton (Calif.) Record

Q.   I am one of the many who have a flat bust. In a recent article you suggested the use of dumbells but you did not tell us what weight to use . . .

The Post

Summer is icumen in
Lewdly sing 'cucu'

Bennington (Vermont) Banner

When the express arrived the superintendent of the local zoo was summoned, and after a three hours' struggle he was lassoed and pulled into a waiting cage.

Sunday Paper

He was certainly the first Caliph since Mahomet the Prophet to wear a wrist watch.

Surrey Paper

The Lomas Fire Brigade was soon on the scene and helped by members of the railway personnel were able to reduce the two carriages to a smouldering heap.

Buenos Aires Herald

For four Sundays in July and August the Pastor will not be in his pulpit. And for these four Sundays the congregation is assured of a rich spiritual diet.

California Church Calendar

Discovered at 5.06 a.m. the flames starting on the third floor of the Midwest Salvage Co., spread so rapidly that the first firemen on the scene were driven back to safety and leaped across three streets to ignite other buildings.

Cincinnati Times Star

'Heavens, I am thirty!' she said. 'Please get me a drink.'

Magazine Story

Freaks of the cold spell
. . . The harbour and Long Island Sound were covered thick with ice and a large number of trans-atlantic steamers could not get in. Traffic was almost at a standstill. In a village near New York a woman was found in bed beside her husband.

Neue Wurzbürge Zeitung

I have been sitting at the window making notes of the number of buses, and the contents of passengers.

Letter in Hampstead & Highgate Express

Mrs. Oscar Maddox is able to be up after being confined to bed for several weeks with malaria fever, to the delight of her friends.

Thomasville (Georgia) Times-Enterprise

Miss Georgina P. Mathie, principal psychologist, County of Stirling, quoted the case of a nine-year-old boy who ran amok with a hatchet in the large family of which he was a member, saying, 'There are far too many bairns here.' She showed how by psychological treatment he became completely adjusted and several years later was working a guillotine in a printer's establishment.

Ross-shire Journal

There was no damage to the truck, but the two
front fenders, headlights, bumper-guard, and girl of
Fitzgerald's car were damaged.

Mamaroneck (New York) Times

Sir Henry D—— was presented today with the
honorary Freedom of Plymouth. The magistrate
remanded him in custody 'in order to get the alcohol
out of his system'.

Evening Paper

The fire, which started at 8.30 a.m., was
extinguished after six hours fight. It is thought that
combustion was the cause of the fire.

Illinois Paper

Marjorie would often take her eyes from the deck
and cast them far out to sea.

Short Story

When a Suffolk fisher-lad sets his heart upon a
maiden, he does not beat about the bust.

Adelaide Register

The Brigade was called and distinguished the
flames.

Evening Paper

'Why are you here today, Mr.—— Lomax?' Alice
stumbled over the unfamiliar name. Mark reached
out his hand to help her to her feet.

Woman's World

58

The large spectacles that he wore halfway down his hooked nose did not disguise the fact that the latter were red with weeping.

Daily Mail

Young men are beginning to object to tousle-headed girls in ill-made, mannish clothes. Girls, it seems to me, are not especially pleased with unshaven, uncouth, ungallant boys or varicose ulcer.

Philadelphia Enquirer

My wife is passionately fond of flowers, and I always give her a punch on her birthday.

Letter in Daily Paper

Mr. John McCutcheon is married to Susan Dart of New Orleans instead of going to Australia as he requested.

New Orleans Paper

Horace picked up a shabby-looking volume. His ear, keen for an approaching footstep, turned over the leaves.

Guernsey Paper

She grew redder and her cheeks seemed to swell under her tight black blouse.

from 'Gypsy Gypsy' by Rumer Godden

He went across to the fireplace and stood with his back to its warmth, staring into the fire with unseeing eyes.

Short Story

'I didn't get hurt at all,' she explained, as one of the nurses smeared a deep red mendicant over her knees.

Minneapolis Morning Tribune

New Technique Implants Set of Debentures Direct to Patient's Jawbone

Niagara Falls Gazette

'Is the photographer there yet?' cover the murder yet?'

'The murder?'

Winslow made an automatic dash for his camera, called us, called the no murder. Finally the story came out. Parties unnamed had just wanted to see how excited they could get Winslow.

We couldn't check this story into her henhouse and found no near Leesburg house-wife but it just as good anyhow.

'If only I had an egg,' she lamented to herself, probably hen walked over to her, stopped,

At that very moment, an old thinking about breakfast. deposited a single egg on the floor at her feet and walked off.

'How's that for service?'

Leesburg (Virginia) Loudoun News

The doctor looked closely at the woman's face. 'It's a most peculiar thing,' he murmured.

Short Story

We regret to state that Mr.—— who is seriously indisposed at his residence, showed slight signs of improvement yesterday.

West Indian Paper

Miss S—— sang the first verse and then the audience all sank together.

Local Paper

Zanuck, in his speech, showed great humility and told briefly of his beginning here in our midst. But he didn't reflect his early struggles; how, when he wrote and wrote and got one rejection after the other and could not even get into a studio, he had to take a job down at Wilmington catching hot rivets in the ship-building plant to eat.

Hollywood Reporter

The programme for today at the Opera compromises Samson et Dalila.

Continental Daily Mail

Man Critical after Bus backs into Him

Middletown (Conn.) Press

Midwife Maria Sack asks us to say that neither she nor her husband is identical with the Frau Sack who was arrested in Schönberg.

Berliner Tageblatt

BEWARE!

TO TOUCH THESE WIRES IS INSTANT DEATH

Anyone found doing so will be prosecuted

Signboard

The man who would stoop so low as to write an anonymous letter, the least he could do would be to sign his name to it.

Letter in Irish Paper

He had killed Nana once and she had ignored it. Too inexperienced perhaps to make anything of it.

Dallas Times-Herald

Undoubtedly the club is the place for a bachelor. It is not right, however, for a married man to pass the evenings away from home while his poor wife sadly rocks the cradle with one foot and wipes away the tears with the other.

Church Sermon

Child's pony, 12 h.p., very quiet.

Provincial Paper

Here is an evening prayer for the little ones, and to me it is very sweet and solemn:

> Saviour, tender Shepherd, hear me,
> Bless thy little lamb tonight;
> In the darkness be Thou near me,
> Keep me safe till morning light.
> To remove rust from window glass, dip
> cloth in coal oil and rub hard.

Kansas City Star

Mrs. —— wishes to thank the nurse and doctor for their kind co-operation in the loss of her husband.

North Bucks Times

The seaman, severely injured when the ship was three hours out, was taken to hospital and the hippopotamus removed.

Daily Telegraph

In the preliminary examination of patients the author introduces a test that is new to us; two or three breaths having been drawn through the nose, this organ is then punched by the anaesthetist, while the patient holds his breath as long as possible.

The Practitioner

Immediately after the ceremony the bride and bridegroom go into the vestry and sigh.

Answer to correspondent

The service ended with the singing of the good old hymn: 'All police that on earth do dwell.'

Canadian Paper

ALCOHOLISM

Dr. C. Nelson Davis will discuss this health problem at an education meeting of the Junior League.
On Tuesday March 18th at 7.45 p.m.

COCKTAILS FROM 6 P.M.

Lecture Invitation

Have plenty of oranges in the house. They can be relied on to keep the doctor away.

Woman's Paper

We charge low prices of admission but they are recognised by our regular visitors as being consistent with the quality of the films screened.

Singapore Free Press

Giacomo Puccini singing 'Michiamano Mimi' from *La Boheme* and Edward Grieg singing 'I Love Thee', were soloists.

Camden (N.J.) Courier-Post

WANTED – position in cabaret; no bad habits; willing to learn.

Boston News

As soon as Miss W—— knew she was to sin, she telephoned her husband in Kansas.

New York Times

The famous German composer, Karl Maria von Weber, was born in Eutin, Oldenburg, in 1786, a few weeks after the production in Germany, at Covent Garden, of his opera *Oberon*.

Indiana Paper

The number of unvaccinated children born in Lambeth during the last three years averages 800 a year.

Daily Paper

One man was admitted to hospital suffering from buns.

Bristol Paper

Visitors are requested not to throw coffee or other matter into this basin. Why, else it stuffs the place inconvenient for the other world.

Notice above sink in Italian Hotel

Again, students often do not know enough about the conditions of life here, the climate, the food, the regulations, above all the high cost of living. Difficulties are constantly arising because students arrive with their fiancees calculated to a nicety and with no margin for emergencies.

Delhi Paper

WRECKER SERVICE – Member's car will be pulled out of ditch, or stuck in mud, or involved in accident free of charge within radius of 10 miles.

Dallas Automobile Club Notice

Cross-channel steamers from Liverpool, Heysham, and Glasgow made Belfast three hours late. One of these brought down the committee tent at Shrewsbury Hospital races after police and others had rescued the takings just in time.

Daily Paper

FINE OPPOSUM PELTS, dyed to look exactly like fine opossum.

Advert. in Philadelphia Bulletin

Before placing your orders in the usual channel for the coming term, we should like you to be thoroughly convinced that our services can be dispensed with advantageously.

Tradesman's Circular

BUNGALOW FOR SALE, consisting of valuable window sashes, corrugated iron roof.

Irish Times

The millinery department will be on the second floor and the proprietor states that their aim will be to always have the latest and last word in women's hats at appalling prices.

Union City Times, Indiana

PEDIGREE Alsatian Pup Pies, price on application.

Advert. in weekly paper

Strong Boy or Youth wanted for mating on motor lorry.

Advert. in Birmingham Gazette

Besides school-children, motorists are often compelled in springtime to include frogs and toads among their objects of compulsory nature study; because you cannot help noticing some of the things which you kill.

Motoring Journal

The word lawyer, he argued, was a general term, and was not confined to solicitors, but anybody who practised any breach of the law.

Cambridge Paper

I did not see Mr. M—— at the Antique Dealer's Fair last week, and later I heard that he has retired from the business and is faking things quietly at home.

Gossip Column

WANTED, Smart Young Man for butchers. Able to cut, skewer, and serve a customer.

Advert. in local paper

The van was left unattended by the driver who went into a restaurant for dinner and later was found empty at Holloway.

Provincial Paper

The half-starving man sat down at the rough deal table and began to eat it ravenously.

Sunday Paper Serial

Will you also send me another cwt. of your No. 1 Ideal Meal. My wife asks me to say that she likes the food very much.

Advert. in Poultry Paper

La orquesta ejecutó el 'Good sabe the King', coreado por la concurencia, lo mismo el 'Frisa Folley good fillow'.

La Nacion, Buenos Aires

At the studios, a tiny baby was needed for a scene in *The Enemy*. The call came to Peggy C——, studio nurse. 'Please have a baby by eight o'clock tomorrow morning.'

Photoplay

Come in your thousands. The hall holds five hundred.

Concert Bill

When approaching roadways are wider than bridges, the accident rate is only about one eighth, or less, than when the bridge is narrower than the approach.

Los Angeles Paper

The operation is relatively safe, the scientists said. It has been tried on about 30 dogs. Five of them are alive and well.

The Post

The young of the hoatzin, a curious fowl-like bird native to South America, are remarkable in having clawed fingers on their wings by means of which they are able to climb about in trees like quadruplets.

Georgia Paper

HOLY MATRIMONY . . . It's a grand new, brand new discovery!

Notice outside cinema

The happy pair then left for Scotland by car. The parents were numerous and costly.

Local Paper

Ted could not raise the cash necessary to purchase a house, and eventually in desperation he had to burrow.

Woman's Magazine

Many of our residents viewed the eclipse of the moon Monday night. The sun passed between the earth and the moon.

Greenup (Ill.) Press

Coo forty-five minutes and cover with a layer of sliced tomatos. Season lightly with salt and pepper and coo until meat is very tender.

Beverly Hills Shopping News

RAINCOATS AT LESS THAN COST PRICE LAST THREE DAYS

Advert. in Midlands Paper

Our 'ETERNA' fountain-pen is a revolting invention.

German pamphlet

The troupes of monkeys are guaranteed to keep patrons laughing, riding bicycles, and balancing on huge balls.

Hawaiian Paper

In printing yesterday the name of one of the musical comedies which the Bandmaster Company is presenting next week as *The Grill in the Train*, what our compositor meant to set was, of course, *The Girl in the Drain*.

South China Morning Post

Fire of unknown origin completely destroyed the home and contents of Mr. and Mrs. S——.

Corona (California) Paper

The Ladies' Benevolent Association held its regular monthly meeting on Monday evening. Mr. Watts made a motion that he would take care of any ladies present who wished to discard any clothing.

North Spur (California) Sentinel

Now Mr. Holland followed the ordinary procedure of having tennis courts on the lawn at the back of his house, from which can be obtained a grand panoramic view towards the Chiltern Hills, which he built for himself 24 years ago.

Oxford Mail

Mrs. Andrews was pleasantly surprised November 25th on her 75th birthday by many expressions of love from her friends. Her daughter, Mrs. Spencer, had a family in her honour.

Chateaugay (N. Y.) Record

The Fire Department was called to the home of Charles Hooper on Sunday for a chimney fire but did no particular damage.

Kennebuk (Maine) Star

Princess B—— wore a white and gold lace gown which she'd saved for the occasion. To give you an idea how elaborate it was, the centre-piece was a mirror 13½ feet long with elaborate matching candelabra of fruit-baskets.

Los Angeles Mirror

Mr. Sagara noticed a little cubicle that was vacant. He sat at the table and studied the menu through spectacles and clenched teeth.

Evening Paper Story

TOTAL ECLIPSE OF THE MOON, 10.28 p.m. to 1.51 a.m. (arranged by the astronomy department).

American College Calendar

One night he heard noises from the terrace, and investigated, fearing mischief, but found that the noises were being made by members of the astronomical society studying plants through their telescopes.

Mid-Sussex Times

WASHINGTON – Nov. 23 (INS). Price Administrator Bowles told the Senate Small Business committee yesterday that sugar rationing cannot be lifted unless domestic production is increased very greatly and that the increase of production rests with War Food Administrator Jones, and four grandchildren.

St. Louis Star Times

Wanton destruction is always wanton. Unnecessary destruction is not unnecessary when it becomes necessary.

From Victory in the Pacific by Alexander Kiralfy

We had argued and weighed the merits of the candidates, and most of us were now for Eisenhower. But suddenly we became concerned. 'Can Eisenhower strike its mark unless the shaft is as usual, a batch of filmy underthings hooked in one elbow.

'I washed your things,' he announced. And I knew at last that I wasn't dreaming.

Herald Tribune

Dr. Guy Suits, assistant to the director of the General Electric Company research laboratory, has again been named one of the United States.

Another advantage of the new escalator is that any or all of the three staircases can be made to go in either direction at the same time.

The best plan is to hold the bottle firmly and remove the cook as gently as possible.

The Suffragette leader, looking very pale and emancipated, was driven out of prison in a closed carriage.

Dublin Saturday Herald

The fire was discovered by Frances Boltz, 19, who lives with her mother, Mrs. Nellie Beltz, at the 2610 address. Jacob F. Blatz, father and husband, is in a Georgetown Hospital recovering from illness.

Washington Post

Widow seeks four mornings house-work or would divide in two.

Advert. in Sussex Paper

'We didn't know he had what the poets call a Chilean heel – you know, a weak spot in the armour.'

Chicago Sun

I phoned for the National Fire Service and they were here in three minutes. They did a wonderful job. The first and second floors are gutted, and the shop is a shambles.

Weymouth Southern Times

Housekeeper wants post to business man or respectable man.

Yorkshire Paper

I couldn't help feeling that my sleeping-room would be haunted evermore by the spectrum of poor grandfather.

London Magazine

CAPITALIST will consider financing Canadian oil fields or will send English theologist to investigate property.

Advert. in Daily Paper

A tough age, yes. Uncomfortable, risky, expensive. But also the most glorious and exciting age the race has ever known. Never have human beings reached so far toward the stars, dared dig so deep in the mire.

I'm glad to be living in this day! Thank God for its constant change and challenge and give me the courage to keep in line.

The halibut always lies on its left side, which is practically white, and both eyes and the coloration are on the right side.

Trenton (New Jersey) Times

Greenland Volcano in Eruption

By arrangement with *The Times*.

The Scotsman

Mr. Firestone argued that his client was a student, had not been found guilty, and should not be sub-hauled by tank steamer to the east coast, and then pumped back into the middle-west and Great Lakes area through pipe-lines.

Cleveland Press

Mr. Barden spoke with an eloquence which sprang from his deep-seated conviction of the grave pass which we have reached, basing his proposals upon the significant memorandum which the Almighty had prepared at his request.

Montreal Gazette

75

Gentleman required, knowledge of shorthand essential although not absolutely necessary.

Essex Paper

We can safely say that there is no repair job necessary on a car that cannot be executed more efficiently than by us.

Advert. in Rhodesian Paper

Don't decide now. Have the set in your own home. After two days' trial we shall call for your derision.

Bedford Paper

FOR SALE. A rarely comfortable modern detached residence.

Irish Times

After being free from Rheumatic Fever for 30 years I commenced taking your pills.

Provincial Paper

WANTED, young lady for cutting-up.

Surrey Paper

POLICE MISTAKE AT WALSALL
INNOCENT MAN RELEASED

Birmingham Daily Mail

Chairman of the Bench, Mr. A.C. Bailey, told him: 'You are now living in England, and we would like you to forget this and live a decent and ordered life in the future.'

Nelson Leader

Add the remainder of the milk, beat again, turn quickly into buttered pans and bake half an hour. Have the oven hot, twist a length of narrow green ribbon around them and you have a pretty bouquet for your dress or hat.

Barrow News

Nothing brightens the garden in spring more than primrose pants.

Weekly Paper

Save time and cut fingers with a parsley mincer.

This Week

EGGS FOR SALE. Why go out to Bedford to be swindled? Come to the —— Poultry Farm.

Advert. in Bedford Paper

The vendor's solicitor will then send you the daft agreement and ask you to sign it.

Weekly Paper

Nylon lace panties are among the new examples of nylon lingerie.
Lord Hailsham also wore a soft silk shirt.

Northern Daily Mail

Sometimes I wonder whether Shrdlu is the agent responsible for ensuring that bureaucratic pronouncements became even more impenetrable than usual; I like to think he had a hand in the following five items:

It is necessary for technical reasons that these warheads should be stored with the top at the bottom, and the bottom at the top. In order that there may be no doubt as to which is the top and which is the bottom for storage purposes, it will be seen that the bottom of each head has been plainly labelled with the word TOP.

Admiralty Instruction

In the past, the Council had felt that the first thing they should do was to get the storm water out of the sewers before trying to force home-owners in. It was decided at last night's meeting that where the sewers could take the waste water without flooding, the owners should be told to get in now.

Bryan (Ohio) Times

Ickes declared: 'It should be thoroughly understood that the Solid Fuels Administration is not trying to convert anthracite consumers to the use of bituminous coal. We are trying to convert anthracite consumers to the use of bituminous coal.

Springfield (Mass.) Evening Union

A new licence has been issued authorizing the use in manufacture of food for animals of any Wheat by-product and also of any milled Wheaten substance produced from unmillable wheat. Millers should note that for the purpose of this Licence, 'animals' includes birds, but not cats or dogs.

Ministry of Food Announcement

BANGKOK,

Sir; for the case that your electric light should fail we beg to send you enclosed a postcard which please send us at once when you find your light out. The Company will then send you another postcard.

Yours truly,

Manager, Siam Electricity Co. Ltd.

The best thing to do with people who write anonymous letters is to put them straight in the fire.

Letter in Provincial Paper

Germans are so small that there may be as many as one billion, seven hundred million of them in a drop of water.

Mobile Press

$25 reward to anyone finding red male chow dog or to anyone saying they killed this dog. C.W. Myers, 834 M, Liberty St., Phone 9267.

North Carolina Paper

There is one such building now being erected within a few miles of Manchester as the cock crows.

Manchester Paper

Quiet, clean gentleman seeks comfortable room where he can cook himself on a spirit stove.

Münchner Neueste Nachrichten

On Monday Councillor Thomson's son will be married to the eldest daughter of Councillor James. The members of the Corporation are invited to the suspicious event.

Suffolk Paper

Have you a cold? Try —— Tablets, the really safe, quack remedy.

Kent Paper

My husband took an accident policy with your company, and in less than a month he was accidentally drowned. I consider it a good invest-ment.

Testimonial in The Finance Union

This appliance will reduce your hips, or bust

Advert. in People's Home Journal

The window of the schoolroom was too small for him to squeeze through. Keith scratched his head and did some rapid thinning.

Boy's Story

This is the story of an advertising genius who works his way up from the position of errand boy to that of a greatly advertised food.

Calgary Albertan

No more than 3 per cent of Italians get any meat. They get almost no eggs and no milk, which they make into cheese.

Washington Star

Comfortable home offered to two gentlemen, or otherwise.

Advert. in Surrey Paper

Miss Dorothy Morrison, who was injured by a fall from a horse last week, is in St. Joseph's Hospital and covered sufficiently to see her friends.

Morristown (N.D.) News

The Colonel scurried up a tree while the dog closed with the bear and killed him with four well-placed bullets.

Pennsylvania Paper

I take back, with the greatest regret, the libellous remarks I made about Fräulein Anna Munkelbeck.

Clever KreisBlatt

Dr. Barrett says these lawyers are so thin that it is possible to see vertically through them and that makes them invisible from the ground, except at sunrise or sunset on clear days.

Montreal Star

FOREIGN DIPLOMATS TAKE TO PRESIDENT

HIS ABILITY IN DEALING WITH THEM EXCEEDS THE MOST SANGUINARY EXPECTATIONS

New York Paper

Tobacco stocks are down. Chewing gum stocks are up. And the brains of the world are trying to leapfrog to some conclusions as to what could possibly replace cigarette smoking as a nervous to what could possibly replace cigarette smoking as a nervous habit.

World-Telegram Sun

Referring to Mr. C.T. Williams, the magistrate said: 'It's not everyone who has the courage to tickle an armed intruder.'

Daily Paper

The faces of the two men were livid with rage as she quietly crumpled them up and threw them on the fire.

Short Story

The bride carried a handsome bouquet of harem lilies.

North London Paper

Dr. S—— has been appointed Resident Medical Officer to the Mater Misericordiae Hospital.

Orders have been given for the immediate extension of the Glasnevin cemetery. The work is being executed with the utmost despatch.

Dublin Evening Paper

A sample of milk from a churn was found to contain added water to the extent of 6½ per cent. Milk taken direct from the cow was genuine.

Essex Paper

YOU CAN SKATE MORE THAN ONE MILE ON ONE SLICE OF BREAD

Saturday Evening Post

Our picture shows Field-Marshall Viscount Montgommery, at a ceremony in Durham Standard in the Coronation procession to Westminster Abbeery, who will carry the Royal ex-Service men at the Drill Hall, Gilesgate, yesterday, ere the Field-Marshall is talking Croix de Guerre. Viscount Montgowho holds the D.C.M., M.M. and Town Hall, received the freedom of Durham City.

Yorkshire Post

Fifth Army Seizes Junction of Parallel Roads to Rome

Washington News

The entire estate, totalling nearly £300,000 has been left for the purpose of building a home for indignant people.

Calgary Albertan

TURKEY CARPET for Sale good condition the property of a lady too large for her rooms.

Advert. in Scotch Daily

Chauffeur-handyman, aged 40; wife Vienna cook; occasionally one child.

Advert. in Morning Paper

Oak bedstead, 3ft. 6 in. with wife and wool mattress, new condition, £5. 10. 0 lot.

Provincial Paper

One unusual feature is a so-called bachelor's chamber with a private bathroom. The maids' bedrooms and bath are conveniently located and are reached by a private stairway.

Newhaven Journal-Courier

January 20th, at Kenyon Road, Wavertree, to Mr. and Mrs. Oswald Unsworth, a son (bath well).

Liverpool Echo

The age limit for Girl Guides was formerly 18 years, but by general request it has now been raised to 81 years.

Morning Paper

Katherine Riddell was born at the little village of Peasley. Her mother was living there at the time.

Local Paper

Mrs. —— requires useful ladies' maid for town and country; only ex-soldier or sailor need apply.

Provincial Paper

HYMN 326 'Stand Up, Stand Up for Jesus!'
(Congregation seated)

HYMN . . . No. 336
(Congregation standing)
SERMON, 'What are you standing for?'
– Dr. Fosdick.

Before its late summer departure the sparrow will build several nests and will bear many little sparrows, judging from past performances.

Mrs. Hetherington said that she had not had the same luck with male birds.

The Sun

Dr. Brode told the reporters he was 'not very impressed with the chances of obtaining 'atomic powers' out of cosmetic rays.'

New York Times

Revolting Police Take Over Bolivia

Iowa Paper

A chasm in the road was being roughly stopped, as you stop a tooth, with sacks full of stones.

Daily Paper

Our photograph shows Mr. and Mrs. H.J. Hill leaping the Hurlingham Church Hall yesterday after the marriage ceremony.

Buenos Aires Herald

Mary's eyes rested lovingly on the little gold brooch. 'Oh, Jack,' she murmured, 'it's the loveliest gilt I've ever had.'

Serial Story

The last he saw of her was as she turned out of a side-street into the main road, tearing up the latter as she went.

Weekly Paper

In our last week's issue we announced the birth of a son to Mr. and Mrs. Gilbert Parkinson. We regret any annoyance that this may have caused.

Indian Paper

He looked at her with infinite tenderness. 'I know all about it,' he said.

She covered her face with her hands and cried brokenly. But, coming closer, he put both hands on her shoulders, and lifted her tea-stained face to his.

Tasmanian Courier Journal

The bride was attended by her sister and Miss —— as bridesmaids, all being very strongly under the influence of drink. VERY CHOICE – James Brothers' Coffee.

Birmingham Paper

But, gentlemen, I maintain we should turn a deaf ear to any other red herring that may be drawn across our path.

Report of Speech

Observing the temporary incapacity of Mr. Lea who seemed to be thinking furiously with his mouth open, Mr. Swift MacNeill filled the aching void.

Liverpool Courier

In 1918 he was appointed business manager of the Great War at a salary of £15 per week.

West Country Paper

'I - I didn't know you cared for me in that way. I've always thought of you as just a great big bother.'

Newspaper Serial

Due to an error Mr. and Mrs. S.E. Ankrum, 104 West Healey St., are the parents of a girl, born Tuesday morning in the Mercy Hospital.

Illinois Paper

The Chairman said defendant would be fined £10 and his licence endorsed. If he did not mind he would be disqualified from driving altogether.

Police Court News

Englishman's Adventure

TIED UP TO TREE

BY SPECIAL WIRE

Daily Telegraph

When Miss Dixie Janice Byram, daughter of Mr. and Mrs. R.C. Bryam of this city, became the bride of Edward Hersey on Friday afternoon at 2 o'clock at many friends here occurred last overshirt of lace. Her hat was the First Presbyterian Church.

Winter Haven (Florida) Herald

GREAT SHOE OFFER . . . **Every pain guaranteed.**

Provincial Paper

The Vicar proposed the health of the newly married couple, for which the bridegroom thanked and was enthusiastically drunk.

Indian Paper

The plumbers have finished their part of the contract at the new township, and there now remains only the plumbing to be done.

Australian Paper

The stove will stand by itself anywhere. It omits neither smoke nor smell.

Newcastle Paper

Why rend your garments elsewhere when our up-to-date laundry can do the work more effectively?

New Zealand Paper

He was asked if he contemplated any further act of matrimony.

'Certainly' was his evasive reply.

New York World

We've got fifty Yankettes married into English nobility right now. Some are duchesses. Some are countesses. Eleven are baronesses. Only one is a lady.

Boston Globe

Mr. and Mrs. A.P. Hageman are rejoicing over the arrival of a mafwpy cmfwyp emfwpy cmfpwpp doing nicely.

Florida Paper

The Chairman said the Council had never paid one penny for the oiling and washing of the Fire Brigade.

Local Paper

This picture shows the 'Blizzard Baby' who was born in a hospital parking lot unnoticed by her father and mother who collapsed as she stepped from an automobile.

'I've something to tell you, Peggy. I may call you Piggy, mayn't I?'

He leaned his head against her hair. A wasp strayed across his face. He kissed it.

BIRTHS, DEATHS, and MIRAGES

B—— & Sons, home-decorators and plumbers, etc. All work cheaply and nearly done.

CLOTHES BRUSH. The genuine pigskin back opens with a zipper and inside are tweezers, scissors, nail-file, and a bomb.

All our season's Goods will be offered at most treasonable prices

The new automatic couplings fitted to the organ will enable Mr. —— to change his combinations without moving his feet.

OUR LOW PRICES ARE THE DIRECT RESULT OF OUR LOWERED PRICE POLICY

Advert. in New York Times

Should a customer cut his hair and shave at the same time, the price will be one shilling.

Jamaican Daily Gleaner

During the morning there was a steady demand for coarse yarns.

Financial column

NO ICE SOLD AFTER 4 P.M. ESPECIALLY 5 CENT PIECES

Shop sign in Baltimore

The public is to be allowed to inspect the Crematorium on Sundays. Other amusements will be found advertised in the local Press.

Canadian Paper

The interesting announcement is made that Finchdale Priory has been handed over to the Society for the Prevention of Ancient Monuments.

Provincial Paper

'Yes,' she said, 'those things over there are my husbands.'

Newspaper serial

To bring wives over by telephone without permit, consult Mr. —— , Marine Superintendent and Receiver of Wrecks.

Notice at Naval Base

91

IRATE HOUSEHOLDERS – Why be swindled in a clumsy manner? Fetch your second-hand clothing to me and be done in the most approved style.

Advert. in Daily Paper

Mr. and Mrs. Wally Burman of Sioux Falls have just arrived at the Lindau home where they will be housepests for several days.

Minnesota Paper

My wife took an instant dislike to my guests and went out of her way to make painful scones.

Evening Paper

WESLEYAN CHURCH

Minister: Rev. J. Flesher Rumfitt
11 a.m.   Rev. J.F. Rumftt
7.30 p.m.   Rev. J.F. Rufimfitt.

South African Paper

VISIT OF 10 WESLEYAN MINISTERS TO C—— CHURCH

———

'Is happiness possible today?'

Northern Paper

BLANK'S MACARONI AND CHEESE
IN
TOMATO SAUCE
containing
TOMATO SAUCE, MACARONI and CHEESE

Label on Tin

We never allow a dissatisfied customer to leave the premises if we can avoid it. It doesn't pay.

Drapery Advert. in Scottish Paper

Americans are offered perfect Grandfathers, one dwarf, one inlaid.

The Connoisseur

In the foreign exchange market, the 6.58½ zip T shrdlu shrdlu cmfwyp shrdlu franc was dealt in around 5.12 cents.

Daily Paper

Try out patent mosquito destroyer coil. It is perfectly safe for mosquitoes.

Advert. in Burmese Paper

He sat there quite calmly, a pipe wedged between his lids.

Boys' Paper

If your skin is not liable to be sensitive, rub the arms gently with pumice stone. This will take them right off.

Woman's Paper

Bob guided her to the spinet. He took his spectacles off his beaky nose and invited Mrs. Ransome to admire it.
'It's much smaller than Aunt Bertha's,' she said.

Modern Woman

She stood at the foot of the stairs, narrowing her eyes and breathing through her hips.

Saturday Evening Post

In addition to the fine work done by the Irish regiments he assured them that many a warm Irish heart beat under a Scottish kilt.

Daily Paper

Robinson, who had been auctioned several times by the referee, was ordered off the field.

Sussex Paper

Len Hutton carried his bath through the innings.

Sussex Paper

FOR SALE – A small bungalow containing five estate agents.

Local Paper

House and shop for sale; excellent position; tenant under notice to expire end of March.

Welsh Paper

Owing to the continued illness of the Vicar, which we trust is reaching its last stage, the services have been conducted by the Rev. ——

New Zealand Diocesan Magazine

Never crumble your bread or roll in the soup.

Etiquette Book

Break the eggs carefully into a basin taking care not to break the eggs.

Cookery Book

To making good leaks in pipes . . . £3

Plumber's account

Like Adela, he had dark brown hair, with enormous black eyebrows, a moustache, and a short beard.

From 'A marriage of inconvenience' by Thomas Cobb

When the wives are bottled they are put into a cool cellar and kept there for some time.

Evening Paper

'Put soap on the runners of the bureau drawers instead of jerking them in and out until they fall apart,' advises John Litwinko.
'If that doesn't help, take the the Methodist Episcopal Church.'

Philadelphia Evening Bulletin

'How can you say such a thing about him?' she gasped, 'I'm certain of one thing – whatever may come between us, and wherever he may be on this earth, Arthur will always remember that I love ham.'

Short Story

20 MILES FROM BRIGHTON
LOVELY LITTLE GENTLEMAN'S WEEK-END RESIDENCE

Country Life

The Librarian reports that we now have in our Reference Library a large number of boobs than has any other library in the County.

West Country Paper

D—— Amateur Operatic Society. Booing office opens on Monday.

Provincial Paper

NEW YORK, March 4th. – Helen Hayes, whose work on the stage was interrupted by maternity, is to return in a manless play.

Columbus Dispatch

It's a fine scene, denoting 'Eat, drink, and be merry, to-morrow we 'Eat, drink, and be merry for tomorrow we lose its spontaneous significance.

Liverpool Paper

THERE IS NO SUBSTITUTE FOR OUR COFFEE SO DO NOT TRY IT

OTHERS HAVE TO THEIR SORROW

Advert. in Canadian Paper

The eminent statistician rubbed his ear thoughtfully and produced a cigarette.

Short Story

In reply to your valued enquiry, we enclose illustrations of Dining Tables of Oak, seating fourteen people with round legs and twelve people with square legs, with prices attached.

The Huntly Express

The skipper spat disconsolately down the engine-room ventilator and stopped the engines.

Sea Story

WOMAN HURT WHILE COOKING HER HUSBAND'S BREAKFAST IN A HORRIBLE MANNER

Headline in Texas Paper

World peace, now as never before, depends for its preservation upon them asses.

Daily Paper

The forwards shot hard and often but never straight till at last Hill decided to try his head. It came off first time.

Kent Paper

Tomorrow week the Canadian regimental doctors will be deposited for safe keeping in Bristol Cathedral.

Bristol Paper

Miss ——, who only recently returned from England, is included in an otherwise strong cast.

South African Paper

Try the LONDON PAVILION, 8.30 p.m. Just the thing for a dull evening.

Advert. in The Daily News

THE BIBLICAL STORY, BASED ON A LIBRETTO BY OSCAR WILDE, RECOUNTS THAT . . .

Associated Press Dispatch

The Concert held in the Good Templars' Hall was a great success . . . Special thanks are due to the Vicar's daughter, who laboured the whole evening at the piano, which as usual fell upon her.

South African Paper

He had the privilege also of viewing a number of rare Egyptian tummies.

Cleveland (Ohio) Paper

Three later attacks . . . tfoytpop poptpop poptp popt popt yopt . . . were completely broken.

Egyptian Gazette

Lamps must be long enough to be efficient, and the average length is likely to increase. Prolonged deliberation at one laboratory has produced the following rule on maximum lamp length: 'No lamp shall be longer than the maximum dimension of the room it is intended to fit.'

Electrical Engineering

The Ballet travels with its own symphony orchestra which is directed by Mrs. Goberman. The orchestra contains 20 virtuous performers.

Clemson College Tiger

Gen. Graham, who likes to eat as well as any man, would like to see a bit more cor bread ad mustard brees served to the President at the 'wite White House' at this aval submari statio.

'Don't get me wrong,' he cautioned.

World Telegram and Sun

NO TIME TO WASTE

PRIMATE ON ATOM BOMB

Headlines in Yorks Paper

Six minutes later Blackpool went further ahead, when Matthews saw his left foot curl into the net off a post.

Football Report

The referees must put the ball in the scrums but not necessarily be rolled along the ground.

New Zealand Paper

For a limited time, Walkers Ltd. extends the opportunity for business women to take advantage of our professional golf instructor at nominal fees.

Advert. in Los Angeles Paper

Mr. Johnson was pinned to the ground receiving injuries to his right leg, body and shoulder. What was most trying of all, his lighted cigarette rested on the side of his cheek, near his eye, and he could not move it.

Look out for the repeat performance.

Yorkshire Paper

P.C. Thomas said he arrested the defendant because his face was beyond the limit fixed for the town.

Manchester Paper

There were two sharp reports, and Radley lunched and staggered.

Short Story

At the start of the race Yale went out in front, rowing at a terrific clip above 40. It had half a mile lead after the first quarter mile.

New York Times

The whole of this preliminary business is nauseating and in *real* sporting circles it is taboo as a topic of conversation. No wonder *The Times* devoted a leading article to the matter the other day.

Daily Mail

Miss T —— sang a number of popular ballads while the orchestra played some Strauss waltzes.

Parish Magazine

Mme Albani, it is announced, is going to take a limited number of pupils, but has been sunk. The crew were saved.

North Western Daily Mail

LOOKING FOR THAT SILVER LINING?

You'll find it for sure with the U.S. Army. At no expense, you'll get the finest medical and dental scare.

American Paper

It is up to the regular establishments to institute training programmes that will result in a constant weeding out of those who are found unwilling to or incapable of becoming incompetent.

American Government Circular

M. Leon Blum told a Press Conference in London today that while a prisoner in Germany, he listened to the B.B.C.

'I can't express to you my feelings as each day I heard coming across the air: "I.C.I. Londres", but it was like a Beethoven symphony.'

Leicester Paper

IT'S THEIR SHOW – Mr. and Mrs. Alvan W. Sulloway, of Concord, N.H., librettist and composer of 'Winner Take All'. She writes music with her three little boys on her hands.

Boston Globe

In an interview he said: 'I have been all over the world looking for the perfect golf curse, but I think at last I have found it.'

Evening Paper

As a matter of fact, Jackson calmly waited to be fetched, and I fear his suffering was not so great as people thought. He dislocated a hip hip hurrah, and was soon all right again.

Provincial Paper

Ten sampans were entered, the boats being gaily decorated with flags. The result was a very amusing race in which the winner passed the post only a length behind the second.

Hongkong Overseas Mail

I was terrified . . . there was the tiger crouching, ready to bounce.

Short Story

In evidence, Mr. Jowett said the idea was that he and the defendant should go into partnership with the hens.

Craven Herald and Pioneer

Sparrows are paid for on production at the rate of 3d. a dozen; rats 6d. a dozen; keepers and rat-catchers 3d. a dozen.

Provincial Paper

Opinions differ on what constitutes sensible food. In my informant's view it includes eating Crean and his Orchestra.

Notts Paper

Tax on each dog, male, one dollar; *vice versa*, three dollars.

Notice in American Town

COLLIE DOG, 1 year old, for sale, will work sheep or cattle, hunt out any distance and stop to whistle; price £8.

The Scottish Farmer

The accuracy of the England bowling was shown by the fact that R—— was at the wicket for twenty minutes before snoring.

Evening Paper

The district of Wilmersdorf was seized up to Berlinerstrasse, while at the opposite end of the town another 12,000 German troops surrendered En Masse.

Cleveland (Ohio) Plain Dealer

At such times of self-renunciation in our own life, it is only supreme renunciation that appeals to us; and anything short of that, we feel, would be an inadequate support and stay for the soul. George Eliot realised this fact and showed it clearly in her portrayal of Maggie Tulliver in 'The Milk on the Floor'.

New Reformer, Madras

By an unfortunate typographical error we were made to say last week that the retiring Mr. —— was a member of the defective branch of the police force. Of course this should have read: 'The detective branch of the police farce.'

New Zealand Paper

R—— had survived three appeals for l.b.w. before the players retired to lynch.

Daily Paper

Round 3. – Both continued to be cautious in the first minuet, but opened up in the second minuet, when both got in good lefts to the head.

Birmingham Paper

Edward Slater broke his arm last week. It was a decided success and many expressed the wish that it might be an annual affair.

American Paper

That hunting and fishing are good in Colorado is shown by the fact that of 100,000 hunters out during the recent game season there were 80,000 killed. This is a record that cannot be equalled in the United States.

Colorado Paper

30,000 pigeons were released filling the air with the flutter of a million wings.

Commentary in a News Film

West End Milliner will make latest fashion hat each month for 18 months for young well-bred greyhound.

Advert. in Daily Paper

The officer in command kept his head and cleverly ordered his men to keep behind it as it moved forward.

Daily Paper

PROMOTION. Rifleman P.R. Shand to be Sergeant H. Cock.

Ceylon Paper

'If you ask me,' said Doris, 'it's more like *twelve* years they have been married. I don't think they will ever have a chill now.'

Short Story

Mrs. Edgar Ramsden was rushed to Roanoke Hospital on Monday of this week for observation and treatment prior to becoming an expectant mother.

Virginia Paper

Colonel Marsden says that the fire was a terrible blow to him for he had spent a large sum of money on it and had extensions and improvements in view.

Yorks Paper

All the goods saved from the ruins was a bushel of potatoes. They escaped only in their night clothing.

Pennsylvania Paper

SPECIAL TODAY – Stewed teak and potatoes.

Menu in East End Café

A chicken thief was reported active on Wednesday night, and at the Bennett J. Dickerman property a score of fine chickens were taken from the poultry house. The matter was reported at police head-quarters and is being investigated.

———

A chicken pie supper will be served by the Ladies' Aid Society in Centreville parish house on Thursday at 6 o'clock.

New Haven Journal-Courier

Plastic makes a new space saver for mothers who live in crowded quarters or who must travel with a small baby in the form of an inflatable bathtub.

Dallas Morning News

Be sure to keep your children away from this poison. This may not kill them at once but gradually they will all die.

Farming Paper

For coping with unexpected guests, it is always a good plan to keep a few tons of sardines in the house.

Woman's Paper

QUICKLY MADE SOUP – Required: 4 lbs. Fat, ¾ lb. caustic soda, 10 ozs. resin, 9 pints of water.

Sunday Paper

When the baby is done drinking it must be unscrewed and laid in a cool place under a tap. If the baby does not thrive on fresh milk it should be boiled.

Women's Magazine

Our morality rate in Fairfield is low while our birthrate is high.

Alabama Paper

STOCKINGS DOWN AGAIN
WANTED: FAT CALVES

Adverts. in Jersey Paper

Practise thinning in winter time and head back in summer. A tree can be kept bearing practically regular crops. Of course, it is impossible to keep any tree bearing practically regular crops, but of course it is impossible to keep any tree bearing a full crop regularly. Wonders can be done by this system of pruning.

Nurseryman's Leaflet

WANTED – A steady young woman to wash, iron, and milk two cows.

New Zealand Paper

My lunch these days consists of a chair in the park and the Daily Mail.

Letter in The Daily Mail

At next Wednesday's children's party it is expected that in two hours 300 children will consume 1,800 sandwiches and 900 fancy cakes, gallons of milk and tea, pounds of butter and a fishfryer, a plumber, a schoolmaster, and a railway inspector.

Yorkshire Gazette

Wash beets very clean, then boil. When done, swim out into a pan of cold water and slip the skins off with the fingers.

Boston Globe

Dig the ground over thoroughly and then pant.

Gardening Article

It was one of those perfect June nights that so seldom occur except in August.

Magazine Story

A full charge of shot struck Mr. Cozad squarely in the back door of the henhouse.

Illinois Paper

Send mother a gift of hardly ever blooming rose bushes.

Sioux Falls Argus-Leader

Mr. —— held that purchased meat should be better than that supplied by contractors, who were not saints. He knew of one case where cattle were actually killed after they died.

Irish Times

He could see a dim red tail-light about a mile ahead
of him. Oliver switched off his own lights and
rammed down the accelerator with clenched teeth.

Short Story

There is apparently very little fear on the part of the
travelling public that their inconvenience will be
seriously interfered with.

Birmingham Paper

TEETH EXTRACTED WITH THE GREATEST PAINS

Dentist's Advertisement

'The nurses who have a seven minutes' walk to
their home quarters, have never had a rude word
addressed to them,' said the matron, 'not even,' she
added, 'when they have had too much to drink.'

Daily Province, Vancouver

TOO LATE FOR CLASSIFICATION – 12
March and April pullets laying rabbits.

Advert. in Local Paper

Among the first to enter was Mrs. Clara Adams of
Erie, Pa., lone woman passenger. Slowly her nose
was turned around to face in a south-westerly
direction. Then like some strange beast, she crawled
along the grass.

California Paper

Keen educated young woman wants Agriculture or
part Agriculture and Secretarial work in Blandford
area. Three months' farm experience, good short-
horn typist.

Advert. in West Country Paper

109

The first few days the chicks were fed inside the brooder house on pieces of asbestos concrete sheets, 3 ft. long by 2 ft. wide.

Poultry Article

Different colours of the same variety of flowers will usually blend well. But just let three or four plants of magenta sweet williams show up near three or four pale pink petunias and WoW!O)?!$§/. following?

California Paper

Jenkins, it is claimed, was driving at a high rate of speed and swerving from side to side. As he approached the crossing he started directly towards it and crashed into Miss Miller's rear end which was sticking out into the road about a foot. Luckily she escaped injury and the damage can easily be remedied with a new coat of paint.

Ohio Paper

As for this puzzler: 'Was it he you were talking to' or 'Was it him you were talking to', Mr. Lewis says the correct sentence would be: 'Was it he to whom you can also say 'It was she I were talking.' However, he adds, was thinking about.

Pittsburgh Press

One of the exquisite features was the presence of the Deacon's wives. We had 83 upon our Roll of Honour, and of these 36 turned up.

Parish Magazine

A PARSON LOOKS BACK
The effect of a Clerical Collar.

Esher News and Advertiser

At a police-controlled crossing, drivers who wish to turn right should wait for the All Clear before running over the policeman.

Hamburger Nachrichten

One of the handiest man around the huge bombers at Hill Air Force base is 80-pound Shorty Osborne. Only 5 inches tall, Stanley Osborne can crawl into tight places in bomber wings and tails to make repairs.

Indiana Paper

The sense of duty on the part of the sailor at the lookout was the most sublime I have ever known. He stood at his post without a thought of deserting it, though buried by tons of ice.

The Standard

Mrs. Joe Sexton and family, of Deadwood Gulch, were guests of the A. Dennys family on Sunday.

Mrs. Dennys is almost confined to her bed with nervous exhaustion.

Idaho Paper

Lady wishes to exchange from 15th July to 15th September, young Englishman for young Frenchman.

Daily Paper

RA RA RA RA . . . Mrs. J.P. Reynolds is confined to her home on Tilney Avenue with illness.

Georgia Paper

Nobody ever shouted 'Good old Albert' to the bearded husband of Victoria, but plenty of people have shouted it to the easy-going debonair Philip.

Associated Press

LOST. Friday night between Market Square and Dimsdale Avenue, Black and White Terrier. Name and address on collar of owner.

Advert. in Local Paper

Double-action Gothic Harp (by Erard), suitable for a lady in perfect condition.

Provincial Paper

The motorist stuck miles from anywhere has only himself to blame if he has not brought an up-to-date road mop.

Weekly Pictorial

Most of the owner-drivers I know make a practice of washing their ears at least once a week.

Motoring Paper

Three hundred emigrants arrived here today by train, 90 per cent of them being people of both sexes.

Irish Paper

In many other towns the trolley buses are virtually silent. Surely it is not beyond the ingenuity and industry of Birmingham to stop the awful screech ours make as the conductor runs along the overhead wire.

Letter in the Birmingham Mail

Another new Order stated that a farmer may slaughter his own household on condition that seven days' notice is given to the Food Committee.

Provincial Paper

The use of salt for snow clearing after an experiment on Friday, was discontinued, because (a) it was too snow was do deep it melted the cold (the weather), and (b) the salt instead of vice versa. So shovel gangs continued to remove it the old-fashioned way.

Montreal Paper

'If it is not worth while going on with the race it is not worth while going on with the race it is not worth while going on with the race,' commented Dr. Saleeby.

Manchester Evening Chronicle

113

All the chemical elements are dissolved in sea-water. The explanation is that rivers have been carrying dissolved miners into the sea for millions of years.

Oregon Paper

BOMBAY – The English Mail Steamer was signalled this morning at 5.20 and is expected to arrive at the Central Post Office, Calcutta, by special train tomorrow night.

Calcutta Paper

Altrenhein, Switzerland – Bucking wisps of snow and bitterly cold wind, the DO-X took off from Lake Constance this forenoon for a six hour fliflgflhfltflftflofl.

Boston Traveller

She proceeded on her way until 7, or rather later, when a noise was heard as of a heavy body like an anchor or a chain being dragged along the deck from about the funnel aft. It was the mate's watch.

Liverpool Paper

As architect and builder of all the property in these roads, I am in a position to say that they are in every way perfectly bbbbbbbb.

Local Paper

While your partner is dealing the cards you should be snuffling.

Daily Paper

Mrs. Alice McCrory and son, Harvey, went to Dayton last Sunday to visit Mr. and Mrs. Carl Dunbar, who were slightly injured in an automobile accident last week. Mrs. Dunbar before her accident was Miss Olivia McCrory.

Ohio Paper

LOST, Fri. night, between Oughtibridge and Hillsboro', a small red-faced Lady's Wrist-watch; sentimental value.

Sheffield Star

DELTA, Colorado. When Mrs. A.S. Glassiter, 82, died recently she on a basis of the acreage planted, was survived by her husband, 13 bushels less than the normal yield children, 80 grandchildren and 25 great-grandchildren.

Staten Island Advance

On Wednesday evening Mr. R —— proposes to take the life of one of the modern poets.

Durham Paper

Lady wishes to travel in exquisite lingerie.

Daily Paper

WANTED – a good cook; kitchen-maid kept; small fairy.

Provincial Paper

Dover – Gas up 5d. a 1,000.
Tunbridge Wells – Gas up 2d. a 1,000.
Lord Selborne up again after a chill.

Evening News

115

The will disposes of a million-dollar estate, the bunk going to relatives.

Washington Star

At a Texas port the largest wooden ship ever built has been launched just five months after the keel was laid. She is fitted with tripe expansion engines of 1,450 horse-power.

Yorkshire Evening Post

Before sailing for Egypt John spent a few days in Dorset and no doubt then wrote the verses entitled: 'Somewhere in England' and beginning:

EFFECTS OF RHEUMATISM

Dorset County Chronicle

Information wanted as to the whereabouts of Mrs. J.O. Plonk (Blonk) wife of J.O. Plonk (Clonk).

Advert. in Chinese Paper

It is scandalous to see these Society women going about with a poodle dog on the end of a string where a baby would be more fitting.

New Zealand Paper

Several eligible sires for workmen's dwellings have been selected by the Southport Town Planning Committee.

Daily Paper

Council 'Digging Own Grave'

SMALLER BODY URGED

Ottawa Citizen

At Caxton Hall the conference was resumed of Municipal authorities interested in the conversation of old fruit, sardine, and salmon tins.

Birmingham Daily Mail

. . . but the petition of Stanley Zwier, American civic worker, who was found this morning shoved under the door of the City Manager's office, will be accepted.

New Jersey Paper

The library will be closed five minutes before closing time.

Notice in Munich Public Library

The Hon. Treasurer (Mr. Hodgson) stated that he was willing to carry on in his office until he had to move from the town, which might be at any time (applause).

Andover Advertiser

OFFICIAL ADVICE – Don't grow your potatoes where they will not grow.

Daily Express

A PRETTY KNITTING PATTERN

Cast on any to serve: – To each pound of carrot pulp number of stitches that can be divided by five; 1st row Knit 1.

Northampton Daily Chronicle

Its lone peal summons the faithful to worship while the others are dismantled and repaired.

Bucks Advertiser

It would be a great help towards keeping the churchyard in good order if others would follow the example of those who clip the grass on their own graves.

Parish Magazine

PARISIAN BEHEADED FOR KILLING WIFE BEFORE MISTRESS

St. Louis Post-Dispatch

George B—— had charge of the entertainment during the past year. His birth-provoking antics were always the life of the party and he will be greatly missed.

Willard (Ohio) Times

Mr. and Mrs. John Bowley are the parents of their child, a daughter, born at Windosr Hospital on August 15.

The Women's Society of Christian Service of the Methodist Church entertained the senior girls and teachers of Yale schools with a tea Tuesday afternoon. Guests were revived from 4 p.m. to 5 p.m. in the home of Mrs. John Dennis.

Striking testimony to the popularity of the Cataract Cliff Grounds is the fact that during the first five years an aggregate of 428,390 persons was bitten by a snake.

Judge Julius H. Miner yesterday granted a decree of separate maintenance to a wife who said her husband left her sitting alone in taverns while he danced with chairs and spaghetti.

Embassy Attaché John Dodge has been assigned to the American Embassy at Costa Rica and will be leaving on Oct. 17.

Embassy Attaché John Barrett has left for his new post at Bonn, Germany, accompanied by Mrs. Dodge.

The Rev. C. Conolly presided at a sacred musical service given at Exton Church on Sunday afternoon. The humorous part was entrusted to Mr. W.J. Hoad.

They looked out of the window as the train drew into Crewe station. 'Hull!' they cried, 'we're there.'

Short Story

Mrs. —— will not be 'at home' to her friends today. PIGS.

Argentine Paper

Pukerua Bay: House, fibrous plaster, 3 large bedrooms, septic tank not quite complete. Owner living in same.

Dominion (New Zealand)

Back from her wedding trip, Mrs. William Crawford Mundy is making her home in Washington with Mr. Mundy.

Washington Post

A jumble sale will be held in the Parish Room on Saturday 27th September. This is a chance to get rid of anything that is not worth keeping but is too good to throw away. Don't forget to bring your husbands.

St. Ambrose (Lancs.) Parish Magazine

P.T. Harris gained credit for himself and for Wellingborough Grammar School by passing in every subject and gaining four distinctions – in arithmetic, French, algebra, and little Bowden Pig Club.

Market Harborough Advertiser

A party from the Grammar School, Ilkeston, of nineteen girls, fourteen boys, two mistresses of one master, leave for an eight days' tour of Paris.

The Ilkeston Pioneer

His mother died when he was seven years old, while his father lived to be nearly a centurion.

Wallasey and Wirral Chronicle

DO YOU WANT A PAIR OF GLOVES MADE FROM YOUR OWN SKIN?

Advert. in London Weekly

Joe lifted his eyes quietly a moment to hers then sat down to his coffee. Without opening his mouth again, he finished this, hesitated, arose . . .

Story in American Magazine

3 POUND BABY BEATS DOCTOR

Boston Record

Nurse wanted; one boy aged 14 months, willing to do own nurseries and washing.

Daily Paper

On Wednesday of last week, two children of Williams Pass, near New London, fell into a 20-foot well accidentally. Fortunately the well was dry and the youngsters fell on top of one another so that their fall was broken.

Oxford (Pennsylvania) News

Policeman Leo Grant was shot through the stomach and John Marcinoak, taxi-cab driver, through the hip, while a trusty at the jail was shot in the excitement.

San Francisco Call-Bulletin

Mrs. Lukes was caught beneath the auto and taken to St. Joseph's Hospital with several fractured bones. The bones were on their way to Woonsocket to spend their holiday.

Connecticut Paper

COUNTLESS OTHER WORLDS

Dr. Jones's argument for believing that there are countless other worlds where living beings are present, briefly, is this:

Ninety per cent of the shrimps served on the tables of the United States come from the coastal waters of Alabama, Florida, Georgia, Louisiana, Mississippi, and Texas.

Minneapolis Tribune

One of these men, a Calabrian named Motta, went to his partner's shop and tried to shoot him while he was engaged in shaving a customer. The bullet shaved the face of a boy who was waiting.

Egyptian Gazette

SIR WILLIAM RAMSAY'S POSER
STARTLES AUDIENCE

London, February 4th. Sir William Ramsay raised the question whether the unfit should be left to die at the annual dinner of the Institute of Sanitary Engineers tonight.

Montreal Gazette

Letters were sent to 665 men. Each envelope was marked 'Important' in large letters, so that those men who could not read might ask to have the letters read to them.

American Education Digest

We made a speciality of gorillas and chimpanzees. They are wonderfully intelligent and can be trained right up to the human standard in all except speech. One of our directors, Mr. —— and his wife are both able to be tamed to live in captivity.

Irish Paper

TOTAL ECLIPSE OF THE SUN

L.M.S. RAILWAY COMPANY'S ENTERPRISE

Dorset Paper

Wrap poison bottles in sandpaper and fasten with scotch tape or a rubber band. If there are children in the house, lock them in a small metal box.

Philadelphia Record

After many years persecution, and twelve children, Mrs. Leah Elkin, Brooklyn, finally graduated from high school.

Kansas City Star

Zoologists could only visit the hot springs in El Hamma with the permission of the local Kaliphat and with an escort of police, since it is reserved for the exclusive use of Muslim women bathers. An attempt was made to bring back a number of specimens alive in vacuum flasks so that further investigation could be carried out in Oxford.

Illustrated London News

It wasn't the proper doctor – just a young locust taking his place while he was away.

Short Story in The Evening News

Headaches? Let us examine your eyes and help you in removing same.

Notice in Optician's Window

Erwen was a man of keen observation. There was something in his visitor's eyes which puzzled him. Suddenly he realized what it was. It was the whisky and soda which he had set down untasted at the corner of the table.

From a Serial by E. Phillips Oppenheim

She could not say on which side of the road he was riding in Commissioner Street, but he turned into West Street on the wrong side. She was sure that after the accident she fell onto the pavement on the correct side of the road.

Johannesburg Star

Electrocution of microbes is the latest dental method. The apparatus consists mainly of a violet ray, a glass tube, and an insulted sofa.

Canadian Paper

To repair damaged tableclothes, first lay the table-cloth flat, with the hole uppermost.

Dublin Evening Mail

WORDS OFTEN MISUSED: Do not say: 'We then drove over the bride.' Say: 'We then drove across the bride.'

Union City Hudson Dispatch

Mrs. George Earl, who gave birth to a 19-year-old daughter is reported as getting along fine. A.J. Dill of Farley, who suffered a broken leg in the same accident, is recovering.

Moran Times, Tennessee.

The bride will be supported by five piers.

Evening Standard

It is proposed to use this donation for the purchase of new wenches for our park as the present old ones are in a very dilapidated state.

Carrolton (Ohio) Chronicle

Baldness starts when the rate of hair fall exceeds the rate of replacement.

American Buying Guide

> 'You can fool some of the people all the time, and all the people some of the time, but you can't fool all the people all the time'. That is the idea on which our business has been built up.

Advert. in Johannesbury Daily Mail

The bride was dressed in a light place in the Wesley Temple in Minneapolis, with Dr. James Brankburg, pastor, officiating.

Iowa Paper

Unaffectedly, Eva tossed aside many offers of movie, stage, and radio contracts, a magnet that was to gnaw later at her heart.

The Journal-American

The other day Sarah went to Victori House to make a speech for War Bonds and not only inspired one service man to buy $1,000 worth, another one $500, but she sold herself and purchased a $50 bond.

Los Angeles Times

The rain was responsible for certain other conditions that made the evening somewhat disappointing to the handful present. Two numbers, however, MacDowell's *March Wind* and Golliwog's *Cake of Debussy*, were particularly enjoyable.

North Carolina University Magazine

John C. Wilson presents

**TALLULAH
BANKHEAD**

**in Noel Coward's
best comedy**

PRIVATE LIVES

with Donald Duck

Advert. in New Haven Journal-Courier

That's enough for now – enough, I hope, to have turned new readers into keen shrdlologists who will send me fresh items c/o Futura. May I now thank past and present shrdlologists, including the faithful Mary Pearce, Patrick Moore, Edward North, and others from all over the 'English-speaking world. Look out for the sequel to this book, which will bear the title, Much too Funny for Words *and will be published in October 1986.*

All Futura Books are available at your bookshop or
newsagent, or can be ordered from the following
address:
Futura Books, Cash Sales Department,
P.O. Box 11, Falmouth, Cornwall TR10 9EN.

Please send cheque or postal order (no currency), and
allow 60p for postage and packing for the first book
plus 25p for the second book and 15p for each additional
book ordered up to a maximum charge of £1.90 in U.K.

B.F.P.O. customers please allow 60p for
the first book, 25p for the second book plus 15p per
copy for the next 7 books, thereafter 9p per book.

Overseas customers including Eire please allow £1.25 for
postage and packing for the first book, 75p for the second
book and 28p for each subsequent title ordered.